Danger and Poetry

Joe Karam
Pilot in Command

Danger and Poetry

One Glider Pilot's First Hundred Hours

From Flight School to Rescue Mission

SOARING WEST
LOS ANGELES, CALIFORNIA

Published by Soaring West in Los Angeles, California
info@soaringwest.com
www.soaringwest.com

Interior typeset in Adobe Garamond Pro
Spine and front cover typeset in Futura
Cover photo credit: Joy Pierce

First Edition
ISBN 978-0-9973553-0-7 (paperback)
978-0-9973553-1-4 (e-book)

Library of Congress Control Number: 2016905821

Boarding any kind of aircraft carries inherent risks. Prospective fliers, whether pilots or passengers, should assess these risks for themselves before and during each flight, taking responsibility for their own safety, performing due diligence wherever possible, and applying good judgment in light of their personal limits. This book discusses only an incomplete subset of all the risks involved with gliders and related aviation, and should not be used as the sole basis for determining behavior. In particular, the points of view expressed herein should not be construed as advice on whether to engage or not to engage in the practice of flight. All provided information is intended for educational and entertainment purposes only, and under no circumstances shall this book or any of its contents be considered a substitute for proper practical training from a certificated flight instructor, without which operating an aircraft should never be attempted.

To my flight instructor Charlie Hayes, a gentle soul and a master artist.

To aspiring or fledgling aviators torn between fear and desire.

To anyone who hasn't stopped dreaming and daring.

Contents

Preface

If your curiosity led you to look inside this book, you might be just where I was in the spring of 2010: fantasizing about flying, still knowing very little about aviation, yet also actively researching what it takes and what it feels like to become a real-life pilot. You've been daydreaming about it a bit more seriously than everyone else; you might have already started taking concrete steps toward that lofty goal and taken an introductory flight or two; perhaps you've even recently earned your certificate.

No matter exactly how far along you are in your budding aviation career, this book may be for you if your relationship with the sky has ignited in you an unquenchable battle between fear and desire, and if, wondering which of these two formidable opponents will ultimately prevail, you are beginning to suspect that perhaps neither of them should, for the sky is filled with both danger and poetry—danger worth fearing and poetry worth desiring. You might also be sensing that for you to both thrive and survive as a pilot will require an equal measure of heart and mind—heart hungry for poetry and mind ready for danger—for without heart, there is no takeoff, and without mind, there is no landing.

What this book therefore celebrates is the story of an inner battle with no victor other than the protagonist serving as battlefield. The conflict at hand being eternally cyclical, its sole resolution is the gradual transcendence that surreptitiously emerges from the ebb and flow of the struggle, much as a glider flying in seemingly repetitive circles may in fact be soaring.

You may find this didactic memoir more intimate than a manual yet less so than a novel. Indeed it is neither; it aims for the factuality of a manual but not for its completeness, and for the humanity of a novel but not for its fantasy.

Furthermore, a manual, more concerned with danger, would censor aesthetics; and a novel, more concerned with poetry, would censor technicals. Our story censors neither and liberally draws from both aesthetics and technicals as the pursuit of truth calls for, oscillating between the two as authentically as the pilots by whom and for whom it has been written actually do in practice. To our humanistic brand of aviators, aesthetics is no more dissociable from technicals than takeoff is from landing, for aesthetics motivate our takeoff and technicals enable our landing.

To better visualize this duality, take a look at the glider pictured on the front cover and compare it with the one on the back cover. Here are two representations of the exact same event, perceived through different lenses: the hyperrealistic front cover showcases my first solo takeoff in a Schweizer SGS 2-32 behind a Piper Cherokee tow plane on runway 31 at Hollister Municipal Airport; the impressionistic back cover reveals the first time I spread my wings and took to the skies. Neither representation is more truthful than the other. One may be more concrete, technical, and useful, and the other more abstract, aesthetic and meaningful; one may more suitably adorn a manual, the other a novel; one may reveal what is captured by the mind, the other what is gleaned by the heart. Yet together these two images constitute a single diptych. Painting both sides in alternating brushstrokes is how I chronicle the story of my first hundred flight hours, believing that this approach will most honestly and viscerally convey what it was really like for this glider pilot to romance the sky.

Danger and Poetry

First Fright

Three thousand feet above the ground and climbing. The clear California sky was a cold December blue and the wind was calm, but engulfing the mind of the glider pilot was only thunder and lightning. My attempts at maintaining the Schweizer SGS 2-32 in formation flight behind the Piper Cherokee towing it skyward were increasingly desperate. Gone was the memory of the tow plane's silhouette neatly superimposed over a level horizon, its tail stabilizers forming a crisp plus sign straight in front of me. What had started as small deviations from that equilibrium had degenerated into ever-greater oscillations, first along one, then two, then ultimately all six degrees of freedom of motion.

The glider suddenly started shaking and buffeting in a rumble of turbulence; I had let it descend too low below its target position, miring it into the spiraling airflow of the tow plane's propwash. I hastily pulled back on the stick, reemerging above the turmoil but soon drifting too high and too far left, with the tow plane swinging too low below the now-tilted horizon. I pushed the stick forward and to the right, pitching the nose down and momentarily reducing the gravitational force inside the glider, simultaneously raising the right aileron and lowering the right wing. This initiated a sideways dive back down toward the propwash, with the wind howling louder and louder as I gained airspeed and closed in on the tow plane.

The glider was flying forward faster than the tow plane was pulling it, and slack was developing in the 200-foot rope connecting the two aircraft. I managed to avoid the propwash by pulling back on the stick, soon enough but too abruptly, and as the extra Gs were pushing me down against my seat, the glider was slowing down too fast, removing the slack from the tow rope at an alarming rate. Frozen, I watched the rope tighten like a giant whip, bracing myself for the jolt. As it straightened, the rope yanked the glider's nose and the tow plane's tail parallel to one another, absorbing some of the shock. Had the two aircraft been more closely aligned, the rope likely would have snapped.

This whole sequence repeated itself over and over, each time becoming more dire as I was losing my grip on the situation. Pitching, rolling, yawing, shifting up and down, left and right, forward and back, the glider seemed out of control, and I started envisioning how this was going to end: with glider and tow plane swirling around each other like violently hurled nunchaku, spiraling down into the ground with horrifying elegance, as empty fields, mountain ridges, blinding sun and infinite ocean cycled furiously around us.

"I've got the glider!" boomed a merciful voice inside my headset, filling the tiny cockpit with instant relief. Certificated Flight Instructor Charlie Hayes, sitting directly behind me, was back at the controls. My first day in a glider wouldn't have to be my last.

Half an hour later, Charlie brought my introductory lesson to a close with a perfect landing back at Hollister Municipal Airport. We hoisted ourselves out and manually pushed the glider off the runway to make room for other traffic, then continued pushing it onto a taxiway toward its assigned tie-down spot.

To be exact, Charlie was the one pushing against the glider's nose the entire time, rolling the aircraft backwards, while I was merely walking a wingtip. I offered to switch places at some point, but Charlie insisted on doing all the pushing himself, explaining half-jokingly that this was what kept him out of the gym, which judging from his sturdy physique I was inclined to believe.

This gave me a chance to relax after the most stressful day of flying of my life, a far cry from my prior aerial experiences as indolent passenger on commercial airliners. I began thinking about whether to return to the world of adventure I had just glimpsed. There was danger up there. There was also poetry. Whether I'd choose to come back or not, one thing was certain: the sky would never again look quite the same.

It felt good to be back on my feet and on solid ground, though N87R ("Eight Seven Romeo"), the glider, might have felt very differently, for a glider on the ground suffers great indignity. Like most other gliders, Eight Seven Romeo has only one main wheel, with smaller auxiliary wheels in a configuration that offers neither longitudinal nor lateral balance: the fuselage either tilts forward onto the nose wheel or backwards onto the tail wheel, and one of the wings drops onto its wingtip wheel while the other wing awkwardly remains high. Having no internal power, Eight Seven Romeo cannot taxi on its own and needs to be pushed by humans or pulled by a golf cart at the speed of a pensive walker. As for leaving the ground to reach the sky, it must further rely on an engine-powered tow plane or some other ground launching mechanism.

When I first opened its canopy earlier that day and peered into the wobbly cockpit, noticing the quaint smell of a bygone decade and the lifeless instruments, Eight Seven

Romeo looked less like a marvel of human engineering than like a flying sarcophagus. Yet highly aerodynamic gliders like it are also referred to as sailplanes for a reason. More efficiently adapted to pure flying than any other aircraft, a glider is as helpless on the ground as it delicately dominates the sky once it releases from tow. What airplane can, with engines turned off and in complete silence, glide for thirty to sixty feet of horizontal distance while losing only one foot of altitude? What organic bird, after millions of years of evolution, even comes close? And what other aircraft can replenish its fuel supply indefinitely in mid-air, as a glider does every time it gains altitude by soaring with rising air?

Charlie and I finished tying down the glider amid rows of colorful aircraft, mostly gliders and single-engine airplanes, as well as, here and there, multi-engine airplanes, helicopters, and the occasional warbird or navy jet. We walked past a few hangars, exited the airfield through a tall metal fence sporting warning signs and an access code keypad on the other side, then passed a few administrative offices, the airport diner, and the parachute operations warehouse. At the far end of the gravel road where my car was parked, right by the airport entrance, was the glider operations office known as Hollister Soaring Center.

Inside, we entered a cozy carpeted room whose walls were covered with aeronautical charts, posters of gliders in flight, newspaper clippings, whiteboards, and instructional graphics. After some additional ground instruction using a miniature model glider and tow plane connected by a length of yarn, Charlie gave me my very own log book and filled out an entry for the first two rows, one for Flight #1 and another for Flight #2. The remaining eight rows on the page were still blank, as were all the pages that followed. I was staring at the chance of a great beginning; pages of unwritten adventures, with one of those later rows possibly harboring sudden tragedy. The choice was mine.

We were only days away from the winter solstice, and the afternoon sun was getting low. Charlie set his aviator sunglasses on the desk between us, revealing conspicuously lively brown eyes that contrasted sharply with his late-fifties wrinkles, whitening hair, and reserved temperament. Ruggedly distinguished, he bore a passing resemblance to actor Jeff Bridges, a trim grey beard barely cloaking his dimpled smile, and low eyebrows enhancing a gaze filled with mischief and kindness.

"How dangerous is gliding, really?" I asked candidly.

The eyes of the venerable craftsman stopped smiling. "Well, I'm not going to sugarcoat it for you," he started gravely. "It isn't safe. It's an intense, high-concentration activity. It's not something you can do casually or ever become complacent about, and it may never feel as second nature as driving a car. It's an extreme sport, about as dangerous as riding motorcycles. You have to fly regularly to stay proficient. You have to be disciplined with your checklists. You have to remain alert and maintain situational awareness at all times. You need to know yourself and your limits, and know when to stay on the ground. If the weather conditions are beyond your skill level, you shouldn't fly. If you're not well-rested, well-hydrated and well-fed, you shouldn't fly. If you've got worries on your mind, you shouldn't fly."

I nodded quietly, suppressing a flurry of conflicting emotions that it was too early to heed. Keeping my focus on information gathering, I pressed Charlie further. Personal acquaintances of his did lose their lives in gliders. Somber as it sounded, this wasn't entirely surprising to hear from a man who had spent most of his life in the aviation community, and it was heartening that he, for one, had withstood over 8,000 flights and some 10,000 hours in the air, including countless episodes of saving dangerous beginners like he'd just done an hour earlier.

I asked whether there were any wrong reasons to want to learn to fly, whether there were particular personality traits or attitudes that didn't belong up there, and whether, amid the cold calculations required to survive the unforgiving laws of physics and the unpredictable chaos of nature, there was any room left for instinct, passion, and emotion.

"There is..." Charlie replied to that last question, his eyes smiling and twinkling once again.

The hour-long drive home did not dispel my adrenaline. Still exhilarated from what had just happened, and proud to have mustered the courage to take those introductory flights, I was still particularly tense and in need of a way to relax and indulge.

Back in my Silicon Valley apartment complex in suburban Mountain View, I sat outside in a hot tub adjacent to the communal pool, then treated myself to the 1999 remake of *The Thomas Crown Affair*, a light-hearted and sensual heist film featuring a high-performance glider soaring to the uplifting piano staccatos of Bill Conti. Finally I was starting to calm down, and eventually felt ready to give more thought to an important decision.

I went online to research glider accident causes and statistics, then perused the glider flying handbook that Charlie had given me, finding some reassurance in the seriousness of the aviation science presented inside. Aeronautical engineering had obviously come a long way since the drawings of Leonardo da Vinci, and human error, though pervasive, could be effectively contained.

There was no urgency to return to the gliderport, but I was at the beginning of three precious weeks of vacation, and the opportunity to delve into an accelerated flight training course wouldn't likely present itself again for a while, so I had asked Charlie to save me a spot for the next day just in case, promising that I would call him first thing in the morning to either confirm, postpone, or cancel.

Still on the fence as my bedtime approached, I decided to take a night stroll to mull things over and revisit the chain of events that had turned my ambitions skyward.

The naive veneer of suburbia was arguably too uneventful and isolating for a bachelor in his twenties, yet its peacefulness also proved soothing to the anxiety of a life marked by uprooting, conflict, and self-reliance. Born in Lebanon, raised in France, and living in the United States, I had been blessed with a privileged education while also enduring civil war as an infant, psychological violence as a child, and culture shock as an adult. Being highly sensitive and idealistic amplified the pain as much as it did all the optimism in its midst, and against a backdrop of heartbreak emerged a strong sense of self, chiseled by adversity and resilience, energized by introspection, and hungry for meaning.

The whirlwind of youth progressively abated after I graduated from Stanford University and started steady work at Google with comfortable earnings and an immigration sponsorship toward U.S. permanent residency. Severing the toxic relationships in my life also allowed me to begin healing on a deeper level, opening the way to higher levels of self-actualization. Fueled by a growing sense of serenity and gratitude, my life was on a general upswing, which in turn powered a passionate quest for freedom and courage.

That momentum had recently culminated with my completing a cancer research charity fundraising effort in tandem with my first long course triathlon, an adventure I chronicled in a detailed report published online. A few weeks after crossing the finish line, I was sitting in a shuttle to San Francisco International Airport, feeling limitless after my recent achievement and buoyed by the prospect of boarding a plane to Europe. Rolling through the pristine sceneries bordering my alma mater, I sensed that, if indeed "the sky's the limit," then my next challenge might actually draw me up there somehow.

For the next few weeks I kept toying with the idea of becoming an airplane pilot, keeping this embryonic fantasy mostly private, divulging it only to those few who already spoke the language of the sky, or to the rare close friend who hadn't forgotten the language of dreams and fearlessness. One such individual was Christopher Pedregal, an ambitious and well-rounded young man raised in upstate New York by French and Spanish parents, whose debonair attitude exuded confidence, enthusiasm, and possibility.

I first met and mentored Christopher at Stanford, where he'd impress roomfuls of investors with impassioned product pitches, gather friends and wine glasses for impromptu philosophical conversations under the stars, or hop in the passenger seat of my car with no other wishes than daringly trust "the winds" to take us wherever they may. He was leading his life as in Robert Frost's *The Road Not Taken* and once asked me to compose a piano score for a short film he directed around that poem.

Now a colleague at Google, Christopher was taking a break from entrepreneurship by sampling the corporate lifestyle at the company's European engineering headquarters in Zürich, Switzerland. When my business trip crossed paths with him there, he was dwelling by the transparent waters of Lake Zürich, amid traditional village alleys, atop a vertiginous staircase, in a quaint attic studio with wooden beams protruding from slanted ceilings. It was in this charming setting that, armed with his inevitable cheese platter, Christopher offered a few simple insights that would steer my early aviation desires away from powered airplanes, toward "the road less traveled."

"Have you considered gliders?" he asked knowingly, going on to reveal that he had taken a few introductory flights himself and was hoping to maybe someday return to the training more assiduously. Lighting up with excitement just talking about it, and recognizing I had only a vague notion of what gliders even were, Christopher played a video clip of that stylized glider scene from *The Thomas Crown Affair*, pointing out the silence and peacefulness of the experience, as well as the sleek majesty of the sailplane's design.

Relaying commonly-held beliefs from the aviation community, he also suggested that the absence of an engine, besides being one less thing that can go wrong, is also what makes gliding a more aesthetic and purer form of flight, one that relies more exclusively on aerodynamic forces and consequently trains pilots to be more in tune with nature and develop better stick and rudder skills.

Lastly, he remarked that gliders are noticeably less expensive to operate than airplanes, making it more likely for student pilots to complete their training and, once certificated, to keep flying regularly enough to maintain their proficiency—an important safety consideration over the long run.

"Anyway, I hope you give soaring a try because it really is a blast!" Christopher concluded with a spark.

Somewhere along his pitch, he may or may not have hinted at the one aspect of his visual aid that needed no reinforcement: the male protagonist flying the glider was essentially taking his female passenger on a sophisticated date, offering a woman an experience very few men could.

Perhaps more discriminating or scrupulous than the average member of my sex, I had always been ambivalent about the notion of seduction, at least the promiscuous kind that playboys unabashedly embrace as a challenge, a sport, or even an art. Nevertheless, the idea of someday being able to invite a special lady on a glider ride had undeniable appeal, precisely because such exclusive invitations would have to be earned, as one would the entrance to a secret garden. Indeed, what greater token of manliness than to painstakingly develop a rare skill that could readily serve as a means of seduction and then opt to exert that newfound power with restraint?

Much had happened since that six-month old conversation in Switzerland. Shortly after my return from Europe, I jetted off to São Paulo, Brazil to reconnect with an entire half of my family that I hadn't seen in 25 years, ever since the Lebanese civil war had scattered us all across the globe. Energized from a touching family reunion that also explained much about half of my own identity, I returned to California ready to tackle yet another test of courage: a 2km swim across San Francisco's Golden Gate, through fog, cold, murkiness, choppiness, turbulence, tidal currents, naval traffic, and naturally fear of sharks. Succumbing to the romantic allure and symbolism inherent to swimming across a strait, I documented this personal feat by collecting from the expedition crew all the footage I could find and meticulously editing it into a short docudrama, *Conquest of the Golden Gate*, which I then shared with friends and family and made publicly available online. Last but not least, I also found time to train for and complete another half-iron distance triathlon, this time through the beautiful Nevada desert around Las Vegas.

And now here I was, six months after the thought of learning to fly had first seriously crossed my mind, a thought that had persisted through momentous adventures and become insistent enough to drive me toward those introductory flights. It was time to find out if I really had it in me to enter a realm none of my relatives had ever called home and probably mostly looked at with suspicion, yet all I had to make that determination were fragments of imperfect information drawn from surrogate experiences.

Did the flight simulation video games of my youth present accurate enough models of reality? Did they offer adequate conceptual training to compensate for a relatively late start in real-life aviation? Did the 80,000 miles I had driven on the road without as much as a fender bender provide sufficient evidence of conscientiousness, prudence, alertness, and quick reflexes? Was it safe to believe that, while an accident can happen to anyone and does not necessarily imply wrongdoing, an accident-free safety record on the other hand does not happen by accident and indeed must imply rightdoing?

Assessing whether the odds were in my favor to survive in aviation, let alone thrive in it, was a difficult task. Statistics and calculations could not provide a satisfactory answer, and it became apparent that the best I could do was settle on a lucid resolution such as "an accident could happen to me, but I won't let it." Ultimately, however, I was still circling around what was really needed: a simple yet frightening leap of faith.

Far above the quiet suburban streets of Mountain View, wispy clouds were gently sailing past the moon, calling me back aloft. But I wasn't sober enough to accept their invitation just yet. Not until I had slept on it.

First Rodeo

The next morning, the weather forecast indicated just one more day of clear sky followed by several days of continuous rain. I suspected that if I waited until after the rain had passed, I might by then have read enough stories of mid-air collisions, wings falling off, and other freak accidents, that I'd probably get cold feet and dismiss the whole idea as suicidal. So I made a deal with myself. I would go back and fly again that day, with one simple goal: to observe some small measure of progress over the previous day, nothing more. For if I could climb one step, then perhaps I could, with enough time, effort, patience, and discipline, climb infinitely high.

As a piano player and teacher, I was all-too-familiar with the importance of incremental steps. An effortless performance with fingers flying dazzlingly across the keys is, at least from a technical perspective, neither more nor less than the culmination of a patient, deliberate chunking process: hours spent dividing the music into very small groups of notes, which, after countless diligent repetitions and corrections, become fully automated and can be re-assembled into slightly larger chunks now as accessible to study as the smaller chunks were; and so on, recursively, until the entire musical piece is eventually mastered.

Learning how to fly seemed to revolve around a similar form of motor learning, and so, with no other goal in my sights than the next step immediately before me, I picked up the phone and told Charlie I was on my way to the airport.

In jolting déjà vu fashion, the glider started shaking and buffeting in a rumble of turbulence. "You're too low! You're too low!" Charlie repeated with the dispassionate insistence of an on-board computer while I was teetering on the brink of terror. I was pulling back on the stick to get out of the tow plane's propwash, trying to do so in a way that wouldn't spiral out of control like the previous day, except I was now doing it too cautiously. I was always either undercorrecting or overcorrecting, and it was barely more than a minute before I lost control of the glider and Charlie had to jump to my rescue.

It was the same story every time. The tow was a nerve-wracking phase of flight where everything happened so fast that I was barely able to process any of the visual and kinesthetic feedback from my stick and rudder inputs. Making matters worse, the cockpit's asymmetrical set of controls was not designed for left-handed pilots, and having to operate the stick with my right arm was a tremendous handicap. Overloaded beyond my cognitive and motor capacities, I was stuck in a state of drained exasperation, perpetually humiliated as the tow plane bullied me around however it pleased. Progress seemed out of reach.

Upon releasing from tow, free flying without the tug of a loud brute felt like flying in slow motion, similar to the sensation of leaving a high-speed freeway for the slower road intersections of a peaceful small town. Free flight wasn't like carefree floating inside a dream yet, but it did offer a chance to study how the glider naturally reacted to my control inputs and observe the feedback I couldn't capture in the heat of the tow.

With Charlie's guidance, I practiced pitching the glider's nose up and down and adjusting the trim wheel—a sort of cruise control mechanism—to a particular target airspeed. I practiced shallow turns to the left and to the right, learning to coordinate my stick and rudder and discovering that, while operation of the rudder pedals was perfectly symmetrical in all respects, operating the stick with only one arm meant that performing a left turn was not kinesthetically symmetrical to performing a right turn, and that each direction would therefore have to be practiced separately.

It was going to be a long process, but things were more likely to click in my mind during free flight than during the tow, essentially like practicing a challenging piano passage at a much slower tempo. Then just as I was getting more confident with my turns Charlie asked me a simple but unsettling question: "Where's the airport?"

With mounting anguish I feverishly scrutinized the unfamiliar valley below, uncertain of the relative size and aspect of what I was looking for, unable to discern it from a blur of urban and terrain features that my terrestrial brain had no experience in parsing. Chilling was the realization that I was sinking inexorably toward the ground while lost in the sky with no airstrip in sight. I couldn't help projecting myself into the future and imagining this happening on a solo cross-country flight away from all airports known to me.

That feeling of dread lingered for a while and had not quite subsided by the time Charlie introduced the landing checklist and the rectangular landing pattern around the airport. I was put in charge of operating the air brakes—one of the many variables involved during the approach—while Charlie handled everything else.

I didn't even want to think about the landing. It just seemed preposterous that I'd ever land an aircraft by myself. And one without an engine? With only one shot at landing? Like the space shuttle? Come on, was I really made for this?

But now wasn't the time to question my sanity. Charlie had just finished landing the glider and was already calling the tow plane on the radio: "Niner Two Zulu, let's do one last tow." And thus began Flight #6.

Charlie assisted me during the takeoff, then gave me full control. "Your glider," he said. "My glider," I acknowledged solemnly, convincing myself for the first time that Charlie was now just a passenger unable to help, and readying myself for a do-or-die rodeo ride. I was on high alert, eyeing the flying mechanical bull straight ahead, awaiting its next move. I'd had enough of the tow plane; this time it was personal. My jaw muscles were tense, my senses wide awake, my cognition sharp. I was angry, yet collected: fierce. Let the showdown begin!

At the first sign of drift, I applied firm pressure on the stick in the appropriate direction, overshooting almost on purpose. Instead of aiming for perfect formation, I was simply trying to keep the tow plane within a large imaginary box in front of me where it belonged. Energized by every successful course correction, I was staying ahead of the game, already applying the next correction and anticipating the one after that. I was moving the stick coarsely, more frequently than necessary and along exaggerated arcs of motion; somehow it seemed that creating large errors myself instead of waiting for them to happen was helping me stay in control. This tow wasn't about finesse; there would be plenty of time for that in the future. This tow was about surviving, hanging on at all costs, and taming the obnoxious beast ahead.

It was an all-out wrestling match. The red demon suddenly banked its wings, initiating a right turn without warning; I banked my own wings. The horizon tilted in the background and the G-force increased. I was being centrifuged to the outside of the turn, pulled toward the sky with rising airspeed. The raging dragon was trying to shake me off into the void, but I was holding onto its mane with growing aplomb. I was a gliding raptor relentlessly tracking its prey, a heat-seeking missile with crosshairs locked on target. With every escape maneuver I successfully thwarted, the cheering crowd inside my head exploded more wildly, and my reflexes grew sharper, more deliberate, more dominant. After several minutes of predatory chase the desired altitude was reached, and with a dash of magnanimity I released the lasso into the blue, allowing the sorry beast to fly away and live another day.

"Nicely done, Joe!" Charlie raved, reminding me of his presence as the world around us quickly decelerated into peaceful silent flight. I could hardly believe I had just flown an entire aerotow on my own—a 3,000-foot ascent in formation flight behind another aircraft! Just the breakthrough I needed. Emboldened, I decided to spend the rest of my vacation conquering the skies. Back on the ground, I promptly scheduled a battery of flying lessons with Charlie and ordered the 600-page set of textbooks he recommended. I was on my way.

Of course, much about the road ahead remained elusive. Even with the "one step at a time" logic, reason alone wasn't enough to convince me that I might soon be able to land a glider on my own, and the mere thought of a solo flight in my near future was simply terrifying. About to turn 28, I was still too young to die; yet I was also too old not to risk living. And though I hadn't recognized it yet, I somehow already knew it in my heart: my quest for freedom and courage would go on; I would become a glider pilot or die trying.

First Push

Three clear objectives loomed ahead on the path to pilot certification: a first solo, a written test, and a practical test. So a cocoon phase began; a time of isolation, effort, joy, pain, growth; a time of learning and mastery. Weather largely dictated my schedule: I flew with Charlie whenever the sky allowed it, and spent the rest of the time studying.

I read and practiced everything I could about each phase of flight—the pre-flight, the takeoff, the aerotow, the various in-flight maneuvers, the landing pattern, the landing, the post-flight—plus how to modify each of these in the presence of wind and myriad other circumstances. I learned how to locate the airport from altitude, how to always remain aware of my position relative to it, how to stay within safe gliding range of its runways, and how to choose alternate landing areas if needed. I learned how to use the instruments, how to interpret radio calls from other aircraft, and how to communicate my own intentions to local traffic. By the end of my celestial vacation I was already rehearsing emergency procedures: how to safely land if the aerotow were interrupted at low altitude; how to smoothly remove slack from the tow rope; how to recognize and recover from a stall, an incipient spin, or a spiral dive; and how to fly an approach if the air brakes were to malfunction.

I would typically return home frazzled from each half-day of flying, and as I lay down in bed reading through the illustrated chapters of the flight training manual, I'd occasionally close my eyes to enjoy the vestibular sensations of roll, pitch, and yaw that still lingered several hours after surfing through the air. Learning how to fly was exhausting, stressful, and at times scary. It was also delightful, empowering, and magical.

Even with no soaring conditions to speak of during the winter months, each flight carried its own unique flavor of adventure.

Flight #8: Charlie pointed me toward the upwind side of a mountain ridge, against which the wind was deflected vertically up to several hundred feet above the ridge. By hovering at minimum sink speed and executing gentle turns along a flight path shaped like an infinity sign, we were able to preserve altitude and greatly extend the duration of our flight, all the while admiring the Monterey Bay and the Pacific Ocean in the distance.

Flight #14: Blue sky and scattered rain clouds had been jostling for dominance all morning. Our flight altitude was barely below cloud base, from which vantage point it was both striking and amusing to notice how uniformly flat those cloud bottoms were, demonstrating a meteorological principle that a subsequent textbook chapter would soon demystify. One larger cumulus, dragging its glittering curtain of rain like a cape, was busy powdering the sky with rainbows, even nestling one in the side of a cloud as a hidden treasure for only us to see. The rain cloud eventually reached the airport just as we were entering our pattern, forcing us to briefly fly through precipitation. Water droplets were pattering all over that transparent canopy that kept us simultaneously indoors and outdoors, and looking straight up we could see raindrops falling directly toward our faces, stopping short inches away before joining others in a slow race back along the canopy's surface. But it was the view straight ahead that was most mesmerizing, because the convex shape of the canopy was causing droplets attached to the front to radiate outward in every direction, gaining speed as they slipped away.

Flight #22: Eight Seven Romeo lost its tail wheel during the roll-out after touchdown, forcing a premature end to that day. On my next visit, the missing wheel had been replaced by an unexpectedly suitable item: an ice hockey puck with a hole drilled in the middle.

Flight #34: A puff of brown smoke erupted from the tow plane in mid-flight as its engine momentarily failed. Noticing slack in the rope, Charlie promptly pulled the release and aborted the tow. The airplane's engine quickly recovered, yet as I pondered the opposite scenario, I was already starting to feel much safer in an aircraft with no engine. I also learned to welcome incidents like this, and to be grateful for the opportunity to experience them in the presence of a master.

Charlie was a relatively private man, who inspired trust without needing to reveal much. There was an unshakable gravitas about him, yet one punctuated with flashes of humor and a childlike sense of wonder that had resiliently survived those challenges life had evidently thrown at him.

He always spoke clearly and deliberately, choosing his words carefully, and with a slight weariness in the voice that gave his bursts of enthusiasm a contemplative quality. "I've been fascinated by them all morning..." he'd muse about some unusual clouds I once noticed on the drive to the airport, the mere mention of which instantly brought a smile to his face. "We are carving through the sky..." he'd softly declare while demonstrating S-turns in delectably smooth air. And when I asked him what it felt like to fly through lift, he'd promise earnestly: "It's an exhilarating feeling... Like being in an elevator."

Charlie had been soaring for over forty years yet still appreciated the magic of it all. Inside the seasoned flight instructor was the unmistakable sixteen-year-old boy who only moments ago had pulled the release for the first time and fallen in love with the sky.

Occasionally Charlie and I would sit down for lunch together at the airport diner, where one of our conversations turned to the history of gliders. We discussed the inventions of 19th century aviation pioneers, lift-generating wings that could glide short distances and even briefly soar, but were still difficult to control. These early gliders later informed the work of the Wright Brothers, whose biplane, before it became engine-powered on December 17, 1903, was first perfected as a glider; from 1900 to 1902, Wilbur and Orville performed hundreds of test flights off the coastal sand dunes of Kitty Hawk, North Carolina, iterating over countless wing designs and, most significantly, developing a three-axis control system for roll, pitch, and yaw. This breakthrough allowed their glider to fly its first fully controlled flight on October 8, 1902, ushering in—at least for unpowered aircraft—the era of modern aviation.

I also learned during that conversation that gliders had not been spared from the dark genius of human warfare. In the aftermath of World War I, the Treaty of Versailles prohibited Germany from maintaining an air force and imposed various restrictions on its use of aircraft, but with no explicit provisions concerning unpowered gliders, German gliding clubs proliferated throughout the country during the interwar period. This started a local tradition of launching gliders via ground-based winches instead of tow planes, and, more consequentially, served to quietly train the generation of pilots that would later man the cockpits of the Luftwaffe during World War II.

Further research led me to historical accounts of the Battle of Fort Eben-Emael, a particularly decisive chapter of the Battle of Belgium, where Adolf Hitler was personally involved with the decision to deploy military gliders—until then a secret German weapon—for the first time in history. In a meticulously-prepared surprise attack, ten DFS 230 transport gliders packed with infantry, explosives, and flamethrowers stealthily landed at dawn on the grass roof of the target fortress, disabling all Belgian guns in a matter of minutes, thereby clearing the way for the German blitzkrieg to advance into Western Europe.

While remaining relatively minor, the use of military gliders did become more widespread over the course of World War II, as other countries on both sides of the conflict added them to their tactical arsenal. By the time young Charlie started flying however, helicopters had all but relieved gliders of their military duties, allowing the silent wings to reclaim their original purpose as innocent instruments of transcendence.

Fusing theoretical knowledge with practical experience, my aviation proficiency was inexorably improving over time, and Charlie didn't miss an occasion to share his approval with other airmen around the gliderport: "Joe is flying the glider better every time!" he'd proudly say to anyone who happened upon us. He was being kind, but in reality my progress was neither linear nor permanent, and my confidence level was on a roller-coaster; there were long plateaus of stagnation between sudden breakthroughs, and it was rather common for a string of successes to be followed by a demoralizing setback. Sometimes an area of skill would improve while another, previously almost mastered, would deteriorate; this became especially challenging once my vacation had ended and I could only fly once a week.

In an environment where everything happens so fast and where mistakes can be fatal, survival ultimately depends on how the pilot chooses to direct and divide his attention. Because of the finite nature of attention, underestimating one's proficiency at any given task can be just as dangerous as overestimating it. As my training progressed, I recognized the need to constantly re-evaluate whether each of the many tasks at hand still needed conscious processing or could be relegated to automatic, subconscious execution, allowing me to redistribute my attention where it was needed more.

Assessing my own skill level and allocating my attention correctly and reliably was possibly my single most difficult challenge as a student pilot. I got it wrong many, many times before getting it right, and then, after getting it right many times, I still occasionally got it wrong. But I was sticking with the training, correcting mistakes one by one, relentlessly tilting the odds in my favor and sharpening my skills, learning that sometimes courage simply means showing up, day after day, when the easiest thing would be to just give up. Then at long last, after a total of 65 training flights, Charlie decided that I was ready for solo.

First Solo

Monday, January 17, 2011. Martin Luther King, Jr. Holiday. A fitting time to celebrate freedom, and a morning I will never forget.

As I strode across the airfield in my leather jacket and clip-on sunglasses, the sky was clear and the wind was calm. What needed careful monitoring, however, was the weather inside my own head, still nebulous from a night of restless anticipation. Though there was no absolute certainty that everything would be just right for me to solo that day, the last few flights had been rather promising; barring last-minute incompetence, the flight I had long been preparing for while also dreading was all but scheduled to finally take place.

Eight Seven Romeo was not at its usual tie-down spot, but I quickly located it thanks to its distinctive vertical fin, a star-spangled blue vertical stabilizer and a red and white striped rudder. Charlie was already there, and explained that the glider had been moved next to a hangar for some minor maintenance work but was otherwise doing just fine. Checklist in hand, I conducted the pre-flight inspection while Charlie borrowed my Student Pilot Certificate to endorse it for solo.

"We'll do a few flights together," he started slowly, "and then if we both think it's a good idea..."

But I interrupted him with a smile, amused at my own apprehension. "Don't say it, Charlie. Let's just see how it goes."

Up we went. Our first flight was a fairly high tow, where Charlie asked me to demonstrate every flight maneuver I had learned so far. This was the first time I'd flown in the presence of low-altitude haze, which from higher altitudes whitened the ground and dulled its features, offering a background against which other aircraft flying below us became surprisingly easy to spot—a convenient bonus on a national holiday when air traffic was busier than usual.

At the end of the flight, while we were in the landing pattern, some airplane pilots unfamiliar with local glider operations contacted us to inquire about our intentions and determine how soon after us they could land. Gliders have the right-of-way over every other aircraft except aircraft in distress and balloons, but things are not always that simple in practice, especially when it comes to sharing a runway.

To my amazement, Charlie maintained a radio exchange with one of these pilots all the while as I was executing the final approach, flare, hold off, touchdown, and rollout. I brought the glider to a complete stop on the runway, and when Charlie finally got off the radio he confessed he had paid no attention to what I was doing during the entire landing. "Yes, I did realize I was on my own with that one!" I laughed, flattered by this tacit yet gigantic vote of confidence from my instructor.

We immediately went back up for another flight, this time merely a low tow to pattern altitude, to practice a second landing as soon as possible after the first. After that next flight, Charlie was satisfied. "Joe, your last two landings were excellent!" There was a pause, then he said it. "Would you now like to go solo? You are ready for this, Joe, but it has to be your decision."

Charlie's offer came a bit sooner than I thought, as I had been expecting at least one more dual flight with him.

"Wouldn't we first need to go fetch some sand ballast to compensate for your missing weight?" I asked, trying to buy some time and expecting that we'd have to push the glider off the runway for a few minutes and walk back to some special hangar dedicated to weight and balance adjustments.

"Oh, the ballast is right here in the golf cart!" Charlie replied casually. I had not seen that coming, and felt a burst of adrenaline overtake me as I realized that, already buckled up and in position on the runway, I was just one utterance away from my first solo flight. I seized the day and made my very first decision as pilot in command.

"OK, let's do it!" I announced resolutely, trusting my instincts before I could fully grasp why everything felt so right. Wide awake and with the feel of the controls solidly in hand, I simply knew that all I had to do was do exactly as I had done during the last two flights. I was nervous, but without any of the anguish I'd been experiencing whenever I imagined what that fateful day might feel like. More excited than fearful, I was confident that I could do this, and eager to prove it to myself. Mirroring the limpid ocean of childhood dreams up above, the skies were now just as clear inside the pilot's head.

Charlie placed a bag of sand ballast in the dedicated compartment near my legs, fastened the seat belt around the cushions of his now-vacant co-pilot seat, and left me with some final words of advice: "With only one occupant on board, the glider will handle lighter and will want to take off and ascend sooner than you're used to; remember not to let it climb too high while the tow plane is still on the ground." Ostensibly insignificant details, each of these precautions was absolutely critical to the safety of the flight.

Without the ballast to compensate for the moment of the missing passenger, the glider's center of gravity would move too far aft, leaving the ship vulnerable to stall-spins from which it may be difficult or even impossible to recover.

Without fastening the seat belts around the backseat cushions, these cushions could slide out of position and get stuck around the rear seat's control stick, thereby also jamming the controls for the pilot in the front seat, potentially causing a crash.

Without preventing the glider from climbing too high while the tow plane is still on the ground, the tow plane's tail could be pulled up into the air, forcing the nose and propeller into the ground and killing the tow pilot.

Nose pointed at the sky like a cannon, Piper Cherokee N9076W ("Seven Six Whiskey") taxied into position on the runway in front of me. Charlie walked toward it, holding on to his cap as he walked through the fuel-scented gusts of the propwash to pick up the tow rope trailing on the ground.

I closed the glider's canopy over my head, then latched it locked. The sounds of the outside world, especially the tow plane's engine, suddenly became muffled, and the silence inside the cockpit was deafening. I could hear my heartbeat grow stronger and faster, along with a voice inside my head clamoring: "This is crazy! This is crazy!" But in the face of my hard-earned training, that self-preservation instinct had little credibility and failed to convince.

I proceeded with my takeoff checklist, reading each item from the instrument panel placard deliberately, out loud, drowning out the ridiculous voice. "Trim ballast. Pedals adjusted. Radio on and set. Altimeter set. Belts secure. Controls free. Trim set. Direction of wind. Rope break review."

Charlie walked back toward me, holding up the extremity of the tow rope for me to inspect. Finding no abrasions on the knots protruding around the metal ring, I approved the rope with a nod, as one might a bottle of wine at a restaurant. Charlie knelt under the glider to connect the tow ring to the glider's nose hook, then walked away toward the tip of Eight Seven Romeo's right wing, swinging his arm in the air to tell the tow plane to keep taxiing forward and pick up the slack in the rope.

"Abort! Abort! Abort!" pleaded the cowardly voice inside my head while the tow rope was slowly straightening. If the voice felt foreign it was because it belonged to what was about to become a former version of me, one that didn't believe I could fly. And if it sounded desperate it was because it couldn't possibly survive this next flight if I did, as it was about to be shed behind forever and left to die on the ground.

I took one last look at the large spherical red release knob in front of me, briefly flirting with the idea of pulling it and aborting the flight, but, finding no hesitation in my heart, went straight back to the placard and finished checking off the remaining items out loud: "Belts secure. Canopy locked. Cable connected. Wheel brake on." The tow rope became taut. Time stopped. Eight Seven Romeo was ready for takeoff.

I took a deep breath, closed and locked the air brakes, then gave a vigorous thumbs-up to Charlie, who responded by picking up the glider's wing and holding it level. I waggled the rudder to signal to the tow plane that I was ready for takeoff. The tow plane waggled its own rudder back at me in acknowledgement, and Charlie completed the ritual by circling his arm in the air, clearing us for takeoff. Flight #66, my first solo flight, was under way.

The world around me was gradually set in motion, with the exception of the tow plane, which continued to appear completely fixed straight ahead as the runway started sliding under it. The tow rope lifted the glider's nose wheel off the ground while I did my best to keep Eight Seven Romeo balanced on its main wheel, wings level, and centered along the runway.

As the ground speed was increasing, the instruments were waking up, and the whole glider was coming to life. The air was brushing faster and faster against the majestic wings, generating powerful lift and making the controls increasingly responsive to my inputs. The wind was getting louder, and tiny gravel pellets cast from under the wheels of the tow plane could be heard crackling on the glider's canopy.

Still rolling more slowly than the automobiles on nearby freeways, Eight Seven Romeo, built to fly, gently lifted off the ground and became fully airborne. My entire being was wrapped around stick and rudder, and the glider's wings were now my own.

Somewhere back on the ground, a camera shutter clicked, forever capturing a moment where life and death, danger and poetry, intertwined ardently; a moment where fear shattered, where folly morphed into promise, and ambition into conquest.

Reining in the glider from its natural tendency to rise, I maintained gentle forward pressure on the stick until the tow plane was ready to lift off. I watched Seven Six Whiskey slowly detach itself from the runway, floating up to my altitude and lingering there for a few seconds before initiating a more pronounced skyward rotation. I pulled back on the stick, staying in close formation behind the tow plane, and as the two aircraft rose above the airport, I felt energized by a thrill best described as that of a passionate first kiss.

The excitement was curbed, however, by the need to stay focused and constantly update my emergency landing plan in the unlikely event of a rope break. My landing options were multiplying with every couple hundred feet of altitude. I enunciated each one out loud, so that I'd simply have to execute the emergency plan if it came to that.

"Straight ahead onto the runway... Straight ahead onto a farm field... 200 feet! Turn around back onto main runway... Circle right onto secondary runway... 400 feet! Abbreviated left pattern onto main runway... 600 feet!" Upon reaching an altitude safe enough for a standard landing pattern, I finally let out an unrestrained shout of elation.

The tow plane and I had long reconciled since my early aerotow attempts, and this once-unnerving phase of flight had abated into a comfortably challenging partnership—at least for now, in the smooth, lift-deprived winter air. My first solo climb behind Seven Six Whiskey remained pleasantly uneventful, and, after the large hand of the altimeter had rotated clockwise four times—once for each thousand feet—it was time to release from tow.

The moment was solemnly arousing. I scanned the horizon left and right, took a deep breath, then pulled the release. I heard the unmistakable clank of metal against metal then watched the tow rope, severed like an umbilical cord, dangle behind the tow plane as it offered the visual confirmation needed before breaking formation. Following protocol, I banked Eight Seven Romeo to the right while the tow pilot banked Seven Six Whiskey to the left, and the two aircraft gracefully veered away from each other. Keeping the tow plane in sight as the rumble of its engine faded in the distance, I adjusted the trim for the glider's best-glide speed; that is, the speed at which it would cover the longest horizontal distance per unit of altitude lost, or approximately 65 mph in this case. I watched the tow plane drop below the horizon until it became "no factor" of collision. There was no doubt about it now: I was flying solo.

Sailing smoothly across the troposphere, gliding silently through the hazy firmament, I was all alone in a peaceful sphere of solitude, thousands of feet away from the closest living creature or solid object. I looked at the space all around me, at the lush crumpled mountain ridges on my right, at the patchwork of farm fields and lakes quilting their way to the oceanic bay on my left, at the megalopolis stretching endlessly into the entrepreneurial valley in front of me, and I experienced a slight chill as I realized where I had truly climbed: atop an inaccessible summit of individual responsibility, where no one but I could help me; atop an unassailable summit of individual freedom, where no one but I could thwart me. Deluged with vulnerability and limitlessness, holding my life and my destiny in my hands, I was balancing knowledge, courage, and wisdom on the tightrope of self-determination.

Every airman learns to prioritize aviation tasks first, navigation tasks second, and communication tasks third. Or, put more simply, to "Aviate, Navigate, Communicate."

In that spirit, my first order of business upon releasing from tow was to execute a few gentle pitch oscillations and a few shallow turns so as to calibrate my stick and rudder inputs to the lighter-than-usual feel of the glider.

Then, as I was beginning to feel in control of the aircraft, I located the airport and set my heading in the general direction of the traffic pattern entry point, above the perpendicular intersection of two curvy roads where, earlier that morning, I was driving my way to the airport as one of those minuscule sliding dots I could now barely discern from my present vantage point.

Finally, once my course was set, I pressed the small red push-to-talk button on the control stick and made my first radio transmission as pilot in command—an announcement addressed to all local aircraft: "Hollister traffic, Glider Eight Seven Romeo, maneuvering three miles east at four thousand feet. Hollister, Glider."

Having announced my position made me feel more visible and therefore more at ease, and I began practicing 360-degree horizontal turns, each time steepening the bank angle of my wings a little more. Meanwhile, the yaw string, a simple piece of yarn attached to the outside of the canopy, was dancing excitedly in front of me. This cheerful instrument conveyed how straight the glider was moving through the air and helped coordinate aileron and rudder inputs during each turn to avoid slipping or skidding: too much aileron meant an inefficient slipping turn with excess drag and sink rate; too much rudder meant a dangerous skidding turn prone to stall-spins.

After a few minutes of practice making turns, my altitude was sufficiently low to begin the landing sequence.

Upon descending below two thousand feet, I started going through the bleak acronym of the W-R-U-F-S-T-A-L-L landing checklist.

W for Wind. I toggled the radio to the other pre-selected frequency and heard the familiar articulate voice cycling through the automated recording loop: "...Hollister Airport, Automated Weather Observation System..." I toggled back to the Common Traffic Advisory Frequency for a moment, to make sure I wasn't missing an important announcement from another pilot entering the landing pattern, then a few seconds later toggled back to the weather frequency just in time to catch the one bit of information I needed: "wind: calm." I visually confirmed that this was indeed the case by looking at the airfield down below, where the orange windsocks were limply hanging by the side of their pole. The absence of wind meant that I could and would land on the main runway.

R for Radio. The radio was already turned on, its volume dialed up, and its frequency set to 123.000, the airport's Common Traffic Advisory Frequency, where all radio announcements are made; Hollister Municipal Airport (of airport code KCVH) is an uncontrolled airport where aircraft self-regulate around the landing pattern by announcing their intentions to each other instead of talking to air traffic controllers.

U for Undercarriage. Eight Seven Romeo's landing gear was fixed and therefore already extended for landing, but it was nevertheless good practice to include this very important checklist item in preparation for when I'd be flying a glider that does have a retractable landing gear.

F for Flaps. Eight Seven Romeo had no flaps either, but again, it was good practice to mention it.

S for Speed. In calm wind, Eight Seven Romeo's target pattern airspeed is simply its best-glide speed, i.e. 65 mph.

T for Trim. I had already set the trim for 65 during free flight, so there was nothing to change here either.

A for Air brakes. I opened the air brakes all the way, then closed them all the way, pronouncing them operational. (I have a special fondness for air brakes, whose control slider, which requires a good deal of strength and precision, can only be activated with the left arm; while this design is what forced me to learn how to use the stick with my right arm, I do relish the advantage it provides during those most critical final seconds of flight.)

L for Look. I started looking around for traffic, both on the runways and taxiways on the ground and in the air around me. The vastness of the sky can often be overwhelming to new pilots trying to decide where to look for traffic, but one quickly learns that, because most aircraft tend to primarily move horizontally, attention is best spent scanning the horizon line.

L for Land. It was time to fly the rectangular pattern while continuously monitoring the airspeed, continuously looking out for inbound traffic, and transmitting radio announcements at every corner of the pattern, preferably immediately prior to each turn so that aircraft pilots alerted to my position would have a better chance of visually spotting me: banked wings are more visible to other traffic flying at the same altitude, and the constantly changing orientation of the glider during a turn makes it more likely that its fuselage will glint in the sunlight.

"Hollister traffic, Glider Eight Seven Romeo, one mile north, entering left crosswind, runway three one. Hollister, Glider." I made one last 360-degree turn, then, with the airport on my left side, entered the crosswind leg of the pattern, flying perpendicularly across the far end of the runway I was going to land on. Runway 31, like most other runways, was named after the magnetic azimuth of its heading (310 degrees in this case) divided by ten.

"Hollister traffic, Glider Eight Seven Romeo, turning left downwind, runway three one. Hollister, Glider." I made a 90-degree left turn while keeping an eye on both my airspeed indicator and my yaw string: with only a few hundred feet of altitude above ground level, I had entered a danger zone where a stall-spin would have dire consequences. I was now flying parallel to the runway, which I tried to keep approximately 30-degrees below the horizon line on my left side while I was making some very slight S-turns to make my wings more visible. Flying alongside the runway allowed me to verify that it was clear of traffic and detect any potential hazards on the ground.

As interesting as it was to watch an airport from the sky, I also remembered the way Charlie's hand used to appear like a blinder on my left side whenever I was staring at the airport for too long; I promptly reverted to scanning the horizon on the outside of the pattern, ahead of me and to my right, where deadly traffic was most likely to come from. I eventually passed the tip of the runway, along with the giant "31" number painted on it that was to serve as my aim point on final approach. As soon as the aim point was approximately 45 degrees behind me to my left, I made my last radio announcement.

"Hollister traffic, Glider Eight Seven Romeo, turning left base and final, runway three one. Hollister, Glider." I completed the penultimate left turn, onto the base leg of the pattern, and placed my left hand on the air brakes, unlocking them and opening them half-way. The spoilers (a more accurate name for air brakes that not only add drag but also spoil the upward force of lift generated by the wings) hinged open above and under my wings, disrupting the lift, creating more drag, increasing wind loudness, multiplying resistance against my arm, and, above all, steepening the glide slope of my flight path. Under the jolt of its new configuration, Eight Seven Romeo attempted to pitch up and slow down; I pushed the stick forward to keep the pitch attitude down where I wanted it, hearing the echoes of Charlie's life-saving mantra: "Maintain your airspeed! Maintain your airspeed!"

The angle between the aircraft's nose and the horizon, known as the pitch attitude, is essentially what controls the airspeed of a glider, or, for that matter, the airspeed of any aircraft, especially one with an engine failure, such as the Airbus A320 that American hero Chesley Sullenberger, originally trained as a glider pilot, successfully ditched in the Hudson River in early 2009. In a glider, every landing is a simulated engine failure, where the pilot has no choice but to commit to landing the best way that he can, with no possibility of go-around, no second chance.

Ready to make that decisive left turn onto final, I waited for the right time to do so. Was I going to make it? About to enter the climactic conclusion of my first solo flight, where quick reflexes, precision and anticipation were going to be of the essence, I dove into a state of intense focus mixed with delicious defiance, donning the mettle I once experienced as a younger warrior, seconds away from striking and defeating the final opponent standing in the way of the title of junior fencing champion of Paris.

"Not yet... Not yet... Now!" I banked my wings for a few seconds, then, having completed a 90-degree turn, brought them level again, and there it was, right in front of me, already reasonably well aligned yet still too far below: the runway!

I did have a tendency to come in too high relative to the standard aim point, but, with over a mile of available runway, I was merely erring on the side of caution. It wasn't even too late to still make it to the aim point. I opened the air brakes all the way, steepening the glide slope even further. With the nose-down attitude required to maintain the recommended pattern airspeed, it now seemed like I was diving straight into the ground, at least compared to my previous trajectory. The dramatic effect was further compounded by the loudness of the wind colliding against the high-drag surfaces of the fully-extended spoilers.

Second after second, the appearance of the runway was flattening noticeably. As soon as I'd lost enough altitude I restored the air brakes to their half-open position and the glider resumed floating forward, continuing its steady descent toward the aim point as I made a few last-minute stick and rudder corrections to improve my alignment with the runway centerline. Nearing the ground, I shifted my glance all the way to the far end of the runway for a better visual perspective and gradually eased back on the stick to flare the glider.

When executed perfectly, the flare is essentially a well-timed stall where the ground comes into contact with the landing gear at the exact instant when the wings stop generating lift. The perfect flare is a mathematical ideal that human pilots can only hope to approximate, but which they can still aim to perform with breathtaking elegance and grace. I could dream of someday attaining such a level of mastery, but for my first solo flight would have to content myself with landing safely if not beautifully.

As it turned out, I ended up pulling back on the stick a little too much during the flare, pitching the nose up a little too high and ballooning back a few feet higher into the air. Floating beyond the intended touchdown point, I calmly let the glider's nose drift back down a bit before initiating a more gentle secondary flare. Eight Seven Romeo touched down slightly to the side of the center line, main wheel first, and I did my best to continue flying the glider on the ground for as long as it was still moving: I deployed the air brakes fully to prevent the glider from taking off again, and slowly finished pulling the stick all the way back to bring the tail wheel onto the ground, while simultaneously applying rudder corrections to remain on the centerline, along with aileron corrections to keep my wings horizontal.

Further ahead, Charlie was waiting for me by the side of the runway. As I got closer to him I activated the wheel brake until Eight Seven Romeo came to a complete stop and one wing eventually dropped onto the ground, bringing my first solo flight to a respectable conclusion.

I opened the canopy and took a breath of fresh air, savoring feelings of relief and accomplishment. I did it! I could fly! Already Charlie was walking toward me with a mischievous grin, shouting cheerfully: "Isn't it easier to fly the glider without that annoying distraction yakking behind you?" We laughed, then with my enthusiastic permission Charlie hooked me to the tow plane and sent me back up for more.

I flew two more solo flights that day, both bolder than the first, beginning with the aerotow. Shortly after our flight formation breached one thousand feet of altitude above ground level, I made a radio call to the tow plane: "Seven Six Whiskey, glider in tow will now box the wake. Maintain heading if you can." To which the tow plane acknowledged, "Copy that, glider. Go ahead and box the wake."

I pushed the stick fully forward, descending into the propwash, traversing its heavy turbulence until exiting in low tow position, with the tow plane far above me and the horizon, its underbelly in sight with nothing but blue sky beyond. Flying parallel to the tow plane at all times, I then banked my wings slightly to the left, adding rudder pressure in the same direction to start a lateral shift toward the bottom left corner of an imaginary rectangle behind the tow plane. I held formation in that first corner for a few seconds, then climbed to the top left corner, through the smooth air at the left of the turbulent wake, until I reached high tow position at the level of the tow plane. I then let the glider drift sideways all the way to the top right corner, followed by one vertical shift down to the bottom right corner, then a slight left back to the low tow position immediately behind and below the tow plane. Finally, straight up through the propwash, back to where I had started, firmly behind the tow plane.

Boxing the wake is a fairly complex precision maneuver used to demonstrate mastery of the aerotow. It had been one of my greatest challenges, second only to the landing flare, but my breakthrough had come just a few flights earlier, and I was now well on my way to flying clean, precise boxes.

The tow plane had maintained its easterly heading throughout my box maneuver, diverting us toward the mountains and away from the airport. Though not entirely necessary, it was wise to turn around while still on tow. To that end, I deliberately drifted to the left into what was previously the top left corner of the box and held formation there, thereby leading the tow pilot into a steering turn to the right. The tow plane banked its wings, and I followed suit, keeping my wings parallel to Seven Six Whiskey's until both reached about thirty degrees of bank, and aiming the glider's nose toward the tow plane's left wingtip on the outside of the turn.

I made a concerted effort to watch the precision of my maneuver, and was rewarded with a delectable moment: the G-force increased to a somewhat elevated yet steady level, and the two aircraft started traveling along the tilted horizon line at a measured pace, exquisitely panning over the city of Hollister while balancing an equilibrium of forces that pleased the senses with a sustained rush of power and control. Like dance partners made for each other, Eight Seven Romeo and Seven Six Whiskey, connected by something more than just a nylon rope, were waltzing.

Upon releasing from my third solo tow, I transmitted, "Seven Six Whiskey, this was my last tow for today. Thank you so much!" to which the tow pilot enthusiastically replied, "No. Thank *you*! Nice job!" While I could easily appreciate his encouragements, it took a bit longer to understand why he'd accompany them with gratitude.

As it turned out, the tow pilot was the same one who had taken me up on my very first instructional tows a few weeks earlier. Back then, when I was simply hoping to come out of this alive, all I could perceive was how much I was being tossed around behind the tow plane, and I had no thought for the predicament of the tow pilot, who was, in retrospect, the real victim in our tandem: jolts in the tow rope were mostly the result of my own incompetence at flying my part of the formation, and through these jolts the tow plane was actually sending stabilizing energy to my aircraft while receiving nothing but disruptive energy in return; furthermore, from the vantage point of the glider's cockpit I could clearly see the rope loosen and tighten and anticipate what was coming, whereas the unsuspecting tow pilot, unable to see the rope, would get thrown around in his seat in a most unpredictable fashion. No wonder, then, that my growing proficiency would somehow make the tow pilot feel spared and therefore thankful.

Now ready to raise the stakes, I decided to practice my first solo stalls. With rare exceptions, stalls are undesirable and should be avoided, especially at low altitude, where they can be deadly. But in order to be able to recover from an accidental stall promptly and decisively, a pilot must first have entered and recovered from a good number of deliberate stalls at altitude, until the warning signs of an impending stall can be recognized intuitively, and until the recovery procedure becomes so deeply burnt into the pilot's muscle memory that, almost like a reflex, it no longer needs to be planned before it is executed.

I made a radio announcement to report my position and altitude, then banked my wings and slowly flew one full horizontal circle, all the while visually clearing the area below, making sure that Eight Seven Romeo could afford to suddenly lose a couple hundred feet of altitude without becoming a hazard to other aircraft.

Not seeing any traffic in my vicinity, I leveled the wings then started pulling back on the stick, somewhat timidly at first, raising the glider's nose only a few degrees above the horizon. Wonderfully designed to keep flying, as if with a mind of its own, the aircraft was resisting the stall by attempting to pitch back down, forcing me to keep pulling back on the stick to keep the nose pointed up where I wanted it.

Soon the stick was all the way back, yet the nose still hadn't dropped, and while most of the usual symptoms of a stall were present, it felt as if no stalled had occurred. The treacherous reality, however, was that the aircraft had smoothly transitioned into a stall and, despite maintaining a level attitude, was in fact rapidly losing altitude. As I slowly relaxed the stick to neutral to conclude the maneuver and try again, the glider's nose pitched down momentarily then right back up on its own, successfully reclaiming the lost airspeed while inducing a sensation akin to driving a fast car into and out of a smooth dip between two hills. As easy on my heart rate and composure as this first stall had been, it is mild stalls such as these that can be the most dangerous, as they are the ones most likely to occur inadvertently and, presenting only an incomplete constellation of symptoms, are the ones most apt to elude detection.

On my next stall attempt, I pulled back on the stick more firmly, pitching the glider's nose up until the ground disappeared entirely. The familiar procession of warning signs preceding a stall was now more distinct. Gently climbing with no engine, the glider was quickly losing airspeed, and as the wind noise decreased, the cockpit grew quieter and quieter. The stick was becoming heavier and more resistant as I pulled it back; aircraft in straight flight have a natural tendency to return to the airspeed for which they've been trimmed—a design characteristic known as longitudinal stability—and the glider was once again attempting to drop its nose back to its original position. But I kept pulling back on the stick, holding the nose high. Soon the glider was flying very slowly and the cockpit was nearly silent. The controls had become mushy, responding to inputs feebly and with delay. Then, as if choking, the entire aircraft started buffeting more and more until the left wing precipitously dropped, abruptly rolling the glider to the left as the nose plunged forward into a counterclockwise spin with the bottom dropping out.

The acceleration into freefall sent my body into full alert. Without waiting for the spin to fully develop, I immediately initiated the recovery procedure, relaxing back pressure on the stick and pushing it slightly forward while keeping the ailerons neutral and applying full right rudder in the opposite direction of the spin. As soon as the rotation was neutralized and the airspeed sufficiently high, I gradually and firmly pulled back on the stick, returning to level flight while experiencing more Gs than during the first attempt. The earlier sensations of gentle rolling hills had been replaced by those of a steeper roller-coaster.

I entered and recovered from one more stall, steeper still, then moved on to my next maneuver: 45-degree-bank 360-degree turns.

Steep circling turns are an aerial version of a ground favorite of newly-licensed teenage drivers left to their own devices in empty parking lots: donuts. Unlike donuts, however, a properly coordinated steep circling turn, with the adequate balance of aileron and rudder inputs, does not skid, and feels quite comfortable to occupants being pulled straight into their seat rather than sideways out of their seat; donuts in a ground vehicle could only feel this comfortable if they were executed along the tilt of a coniform depression into the ground.

While donuts are of no serious use to the motorist, steep circling turns are of prime importance to the glider pilot. As for pilots of powered airplanes, they too may wish to maintain a turn indefinitely in order to practice their turning skills or to fulfill forbidden donut fantasies, but in practice they rarely have a use for turns beyond 180 degrees, and stationary circling tends to simply waste fuel. To the glider pilot, on the other hand, stationary circling is the magical incantation which, when timed and adjusted skillfully, allows fuel to be created, so to speak, in mid-flight and literally out of thin air! Holding a tight turn indefinitely is indeed a prerequisite toward mastering the mysterious art of thermalling—the ability to climb inside those narrow, turbulent columns of rising air that I had yet to encounter but was promised existed outside the winter months.

The more steeply the wings are banked, the smaller the turn radius, and the more likely the circular flight path will fit inside the core of the thermal, vertically expanding the stationary circling pattern into a skyward helix. Another consequence of steepening the bank, however, is that the glider sinks faster as the angle of bank increases; beyond 45 degrees of bank the circles are tight but the sink rate may be greater than the thermal's rate of ascent, which would result in a counterproductive groundward helix (potentially worsening into a spiral dive hazardous to occupants and the structural integrity of the aircraft). For those reasons, a thermalling maneuver is often best initiated with 45 degrees of bank, allowing for subsequent adjustments as the width and strength of the thermal become apparent.

A pilot executes a turn—any turn—by first banking the wings with coordinated aileron and rudder inputs; then, once the desired angle of bank is reached, the pilot resets these controls to neutral while simultaneously pulling back on the stick to lift the aircraft into the turn (in this stable configuration, the nose can keep scurrying along the horizon indefinitely with only minimal corrections); finally, to exit the turn, the pilot gradually releases the back pressure on the stick while removing the bank from the wings with coordinated aileron and rudder inputs, bringing these controls back to neutral as soon as the aircraft is once again flying straight and level.

I entered and exited a few turns using this easily described but difficult to master procedure. Alternating between a right turn and a left turn, each time I steepened the bank angle a little more, until I felt comfortable banking the wings a full 45 degrees, at which point I and the rest of the aircraft weighed approximately 1.4 times our usual weight. (Had the bank been further steepened to 60 degrees, we would have weighed exactly twice our usual weight.) I was circling with 45 degrees of bank to the right, and the ground now appeared and felt as much off to my right side as it was under me, such that it could almost be thought of as a vertical wall rather than a horizontal surface. By simply swiveling my head to the right I could now clearly and effortlessly see those ground features immediately below the glider, which was impossible to do in level flight despite my best craning efforts.

Slowly spinning under me were patches of semi-rural suburbs scattered around the city of Hollister. My circles turned into S-shapes, infinity signs, and other expressive figures, and with each maneuver I experienced at once more control and more abandon. Overcome with joy, with heart and mind in perfect harmony, I was on a magic carpet ride, hovering low enough to clearly identify the roofs and back-yard pools of individual houses nestled around cul-de-sacs, horse corrals, farm fields, and cherry orchards. Less than 2,000 feet above the earth, I was so close, yet so silent, remaining unheard and unseen by terrestrial beings going about their daily lives, save perhaps a child or a dreamer who might have felt so inspired to gaze skyward just in time to witness the stealthy exuberance of a glider that danced like no one was watching.

First Test

The completion of my first solo flights catapulted me into a celebratory high that might have lasted longer than a few days had I not needed to continue my training without much interruption. Indeed I was still inexperienced enough that staying on the ground for even just a few days was enough to cause my flight proficiency and confidence to regress markedly, and it was with a mix of envy and hope that I kept puzzling over how more seasoned pilots could afford to take several months off from flying and then return to the sky with their skills mostly intact.

It had only been five days since my first solo, yet as I returned to the airfield and approached the glider, the ritualistic imperatives of thoroughly conducting the pre-flight inspection and mentally rehearsing all the flight procedures were quick to remind me that the miracle of flight is built upon a vulnerable chain of mechanical and human factors—each a potential point of failure—required to all work together without error, or at least with enough margins and with enough redundancy between them to prevent a single error from turning into disaster. These gloomy considerations made it difficult to internalize my recent achievement, which increasingly felt like a distant memory that bore no relevance to the daunting challenges ahead.

As I was stepping into the next phase of my flight training with renewed apprehension, the gliderport nevertheless had a more auspicious message in store. Eight Seven Romeo wasn't tied down to its usual concrete base, but was instead stationed eagerly close to the runway and resting on lush green grass. As I got nearer I realized that its fuselage had been entirely repainted and was now shining with glorious bright white. Then, just as I was about to go through my checklists, an airman walked by and noticed cheerfully: "You have a passenger!" His finger was pointing at the curved surface of the glider's nose, where, red and black against the white background, a ladybug had just landed.

Alternating between dual instruction and solo flights, I continued to refine and solidify my piloting skills over the next several weeks as my focus also shifted to a different hurdle: the written test.

More important than passing the actual test was gaining a genuine understanding of the underlying material, a vast interdisciplinary body of aeronautical knowledge spanning numerous areas that all come together to influence the safety, quality, and joy of flight. Bringing together the fields of psychology, physiology, mathematics, engineering, mechanics, aerodynamics, meteorology, cartography, and many more, this course had something for everyone and was a generalist's all-you-can-eat buffet.

Elevating theory to the realm of the eminently practical, and with so much at stake, almost no bit of information ever felt too trivial to learn, whether it be the interpretation of a symbol on an aeronautical chart, that of an airport marking on the ground, or that of a cloud in the sky. I gradually became aware of forces at work everywhere, and of their surrounding natural constraints, design limitations, or legal regulations. In my mind's eye, the monolithic unity of the sky dissolved into man-made geometrical airspace partitions, and out of its transparent blueness, out of its deceptive tranquility, emerged all the invisible chaotic energies that made soaring possible and challenging: air masses traversing the heavens like giant ghosts, skating up capricious terrain, colliding with one another, boiling their way up the atmosphere, or oscillating along shock wave harmonics.

It was just I and the books, moving forward through this independent study at my own pace, yet with a looming deadline in sight that eventually forced me to focus my effort in a more targeted way. After reading the textbooks from cover to cover, I read them a second time all over again, taking a closer look and trying to more actively recall information, with the help of review questions at the end of every chapter, along with exam preparation guides sampling the more comprehensive bank of hundreds of multiple-choice questions, from which 60 or close variants thereof would come up on test day.

I passed the written test with a perfect score, and upon walking out of the computer-based test center immediately called Charlie to share the good news. Of course much of all that newly acquired aeronautical knowledge was not yet decisively stored in my long-term memory, and some of it would quickly fade and require further reviews spaced out over time. Still, the short-term goal was met with flying colors and positioned me well for the upcoming practical test (also known as "the checkride"), whose oral evaluation portion typically dwells with greater scrutiny on areas where knowledge fell short in the written test.

Charlie helped me schedule my checkride with the local Designated Pilot Examiner, Dave Morss, whose commitments with the Federal Aviation Administration were only a small part of his aeronautical activities. Indeed it might have been a mistake researching the man before meeting him, as his aviation career appeared incredibly intimidating.

Not only were his total flight hours north of 27,000 in a wide variety of aircraft that included warbirds and jets he'd fly at aerobatic air shows and competitive air races, but he was also a test pilot who regularly flew aircraft that had never been flown before, many of them homebuilt by amateurs. It was good to learn, however, that this daredevil career had its start in gliders. After watching a cockpit-view video of Dave smoothly landing an aircraft that had just experienced an unsettlingly violent propeller failure, I was also reassured to hear his very human take on the event in a subsequent interview, where he recalled remaining calm during the emergency yet later experiencing nausea on the ground upon hearing the sound of the prop failure being replayed on tape by fellow airmen.

Dave proved just as approachable when I shook hands with him on the day of my scheduled checkride, even though that first encounter turned out unexpectedly brief: the cloud ceiling was very low that morning, and while I was still wondering whether there might still be a chance for it to clear up, Dave was confident we'd be better off rescheduling. Updating his digital calendar on the fly, he was in and out the glider operations office in no time, leaving me a bit disappointed that I had worked myself up to the big day, woken up especially early, and driven all the way to the airport for nothing. Frustration quickly turned to relief however, as I admitted to myself that the weather inside my head that morning was just as cloudy as the one outdoors, and that another week of anticipation also meant another week of preparation, along with a chance to be better rested for a test that was financially and psychologically rather expensive to fail.

Countless other test experiences had taught me that a refreshingly stimulating change of scenery the night before a stressful hurdle can sometimes be a wise choice. In that spirit, along with the desire to sleep in a little longer and not have to worry about an early morning drive, I decided to spend the night before my checkride as close as possible to the airport.

After a few late-afternoon takeoffs and landings and some final words of advice from Charlie, I checked in at a motel conveniently located mere seconds away from the airport entrance, then treated myself to a local steakhouse, in whose cozy warm-lit booths I spent a couple of hours reviewing the notes from my flight journal and skimming through the textbooks one last time. I had the small-town restaurant entirely to myself, save for a few Saturday night patrons filtering in and out of a dimmer side room with upbeat old-school DJ music and a full bar lined with colorful potions. There was just the right amount of human presence to muffle anxiety away while allowing for a more quiet, purposeful confidence to emerge. At one point someone came closer to my table to inquire about my studies, and I gladly offered some insights into the secret world of glider pilots I was hoping to prove myself worthy of at long last.

"There you are! We were wondering where you'd disappeared!" exclaimed Charlie with playful impatience as I walked into the glider operations office after absenting myself to print the daily weather charts from a painfully slow printer in the building next door. I was convinced I was still quite early for my morning appointment, so why was Charlie making me feel like I was late for it? And why was Dave Morss nonchalantly sitting in conversation with him as if he'd been waiting for a long time?

After a moment of mild panic spent second-guessing the accuracy of my wristwatch, I came to realize that Dave was simply done early with the checkride scheduled prior to mine (with a transition pilot already certificated and experienced in powered airplanes, and for whom the add-on glider rating was likely just a formality), and he was ready to start with me whenever I was.

I hurried into the friendly side room where Charlie and I had sat so many times for flight briefings and debriefings, and I proceeded to quietly arrange my material on the table while the previous examinee was collecting his. Moments later, Dave Morss and I were alone in the room together, sitting opposite each other, and the ground portion of the checkride began.

"Even though you are being evaluated today, you are the pilot in command," Dave began. "You have the final word on the operation of the glider, and if at any point I ask you to do something that you otherwise would not do if the request came from a regular passenger, then say so and don't do it. On one occasion however, I will briefly take over the controls to put slack in the tow rope and then let you recover from this, if you can; failure to pull the release if needed would cause you to fail the checkride."

Dave then asked to see my written test results, and took a moment to muse over my perfect score, congratulating me and adding that "this isn't common." He then confided that the previous examinee had actually failed his checkride within the very first minute of flight: Dave had simulated a rope break emergency by pulling the release while the glider was still below 200 feet above ground, and the examinee, instead of landing straight ahead on the remainder of the runway as safety dictated and as he had said he would, initiated a 180-degree turn dangerous enough to compel Dave to take control of the glider and land it himself.

While my solid written test results seemed to have put me in Dave's good graces and would potentially shorten the barrage of questions that was about to begin, it was now quite clear, if there were any doubts remaining, that the practical portion of the checkride would be anything but a mere formality.

"What's the weather like today?" Dave asked rather casually while fully expecting an elaborate answer that would draw from cryptic aviation reports and make the weather channel sound like small talk. Questions went on: "How do you determine whether a glider is fit to fly?" "May I see the weight and balance calculation you prepared for our flight together today?" "What are the in-flight oxygen requirements?" "What would you need if you landed at an airport with no tow planes?" "How would you plan a cross-country flight?"

I provided satisfactory answers to each question, all the while acutely aware that my knowledge was still largely coming from textbooks and hearsay rather than first-hand experience. With feigned confidence I spoke of altitudes I had not yet climbed to, distances I had not yet covered, scenarios I had not yet experienced, and responsibilities I had not yet carried. Dave knew that too of course, yet he played along and treated our exchange like a collaborative conversation between two airmen contributing equally to one another. He would listen almost as if I were teaching him new things, occasionally jumping in to complete my answers with additional precisions or tidbits of personal wisdom he had acquired over the years.

While much of what we discussed was not going to be immediately relevant to the checkride, all of it was in the cards for a not-so-distant future that I was aiming to unlock and live through, and it was important to the two of us that I be well-equipped for it.

"Let's go fly!" Dave eventually announced, rising from his chair. As we walked toward the airfield, he asked which runway I was planning to use and what my emergency plan would be in the event of a premature termination of tow, actual or simulated.

Whenever possible, it is generally best to take off facing directly into the wind: first, because the control surfaces (rudder, ailerons, elevator) of both the tow plane and the glider become responsive sooner during the ground roll; second, because both aircraft reach their liftoff airspeeds at lower ground speeds, which means a shorter ground roll using a smaller amount of runway; third, because once airborne, the climb angle relative to the ground is steeper, making it less likely that the aircraft tandem would end up far from the airport while still too low for the glider to be able to return to it in an emergency.

On the morning of my checkride, however, the wind was still too light and variable to favor any particular runway, so I told Dave that we might as well use runway 31, given that it was the longest, presented the safest emergency landing options, and happened to be the default active runway. I outlined an emergency plan contingent upon various altitudes and configurations, and added that I would restate it in real-time during our ascent.

At that point we had reached Eight Seven Romeo, and Dave let me conduct the preflight inspection while he stepped away so as not to distract me. A few minutes later, when the golf cart came to hook up the glider for taxi, Dave offered to walk the wing while I could get seated inside the glider and begin the takeoff checklist.

"Pawnee Niner Two Zulu taking runway 24 for glider hook-up," the tow pilot announced on the radio, unexpectedly going against my yet-uncommunicated intent to take off from runway 31. Complicating things further, the wind had begun to pick up and, judging from the windsocks, was now clearly favoring 31; taking off from runway 24 therefore meant taking off with a crosswind component from the right, which was a more complex procedure than a straight-into-the-wind upwind takeoff. The tow pilot probably had good reason to select runway 24 however, as 24 was typically used for glider tows whenever 31 got too busy with power traffic. I decided to go along with the tow pilot's judgment call and not explicitly request runway 31. Dave was already pressing me however, asking how this change of plans would alter my takeoff procedure and my emergency plan.

A crosswind from the right would push against the tail's vertical stabilizer, thereby weathervaning the glider into a right turn—an effect that needed to be countered by applying left rudder. At the same time, the wind would also get under the right wing and roll the glider to the left—an effect that needed to be countered by applying right aileron to lower the right wing. I told Dave that I would therefore begin the ground roll in this "cross-controlled" left-rudder, right-stick configuration.

I also adjusted the emergency plan, pointing out that in the event of a rope break between 200 and 400 feet, the 180-degree turn back to the runway would preferably be performed toward the right, into the wind, to avoid drifting downwind of the runway during the turn. And of course, as with every takeoff, I would also need to maintain situational awareness and monitor, both visually and on the radio, any traffic that might conflict with my emergency plan.

Flight #121 was under way. Eight Seven Romeo lifted off the ground as I nervously readied myself for Dave to pull the same trick he had used on the previous examinee. Yet while I was worrying about my passenger possibly mis-behaving, the glider was already yielding to the crosswind coming from the right, and by the time the tow plane finally became airborne the glider had already drifted behind it by a good 15 to 20 degrees to the left: still learning how to properly read the windsocks, and likely influenced by the Automated Weather Observation System reporting calm wind as recently as five minutes earlier, I had obviously underestimated the strength of the wind and ought to have crossed the controls more aggressively. Unfortunately, that lateral drift was not my only oversight, as the glider had also ballooned a little high above the tow plane when it should have remained at the same altitude.

While these two deviations remained within the margins of safety, this closely scrutinized takeoff was clearly not one of my finest. The only thing left to do was attempt to preempt criticism with a grunt of dissatisfaction and a head shake of my own.

With every hundred feet of altitude gained I called out the updated emergency landing plan, with the wince of anticipation on my face fading gradually as we climbed. We eventually reached the normal pattern altitude, one thousand feet above ground, without Dave having pulled the release. Instead, he requested that I box the wake. I communicated my intention to the tow pilot then proceeded with the maneuver, tracing a rather precise square, with the exception of one corner where I briefly touched the wake before making a quick correction.

Dave was satisfied, and asked for a 180-degree steering turn. I drifted to the left and banked my wings to the right as soon as the tow plane did so, but, having failed to pick a reference point on the horizon, was unsure where to complete my turn and as a result overshot somewhat, admitting to Dave that my turn was closer to 270 degrees than 180. "Close enough," he said, seemingly more interested in his next challenge.

"I have the glider," he went on, taking the controls.

"Your glider," I assented, relinquishing the controls.

Simulating what might happen naturally in a turbulent tow, Dave was about to artificially introduce some slack in the tow rope, by first climbing up high behind the tow plane, then converting the energy from that extra altitude into airspeed by quickly diving back down to the altitude of the tow plane, simultaneously moving forward closer to it. Except that Dave executed that maneuver much more aggressively than I had ever experienced it in my training; to start with, he didn't shift the glider off to the side nearly as much as Charlie did, which made it more difficult to keep the tow plane in sight; most jarring however was how much more decisively he entered the climb, taking the glider up much faster and much higher above the tow plane.

Unpleasantly reminiscent of my very first tows, our quickly deteriorating flight formation was setting off alarm bells in my body and in my mind, reviving echoes of Dave's mysteriously emphasized warning, earlier on the ground, that failing to release if the slack rope procedure became unsafe would be grounds for a checkride failure. We were now so high up that the tow plane, hiding somewhere below the glider's nose, had completely disappeared from my line of sight, and though Dave was still formally in control of the aircraft, without warning I pulled the release.

The clank of the release ushered into the cockpit a sudden wave of awkwardness, and the post-tow silence, ordinarily so soothing, was deafening.

"Wh...?" Dave stammered in puzzlement after a split-second that sounded like an eternity.

"Oh no..." I thought to myself as I realized that this hadn't been some sort of test. I rushed to defend my action: "I could no longer see the tow plane!" I pleaded earnestly.

"Well, I could still see it..." Dave countered, understandably frustrated.

I felt like I had just cheated my way out of being evaluated of an important item, and believed that I had either just failed the checkride, or that Dave was now going to try his best to make sure that I did.

"Alright, moving on..." I declared in a bid to shrug off this misunderstanding, while simultaneously creeping back onto the controls and reclaiming them from Dave via subtle pressure on the stick and rudder rather than by explicit verbal agreement. "Tow plane in sight, dropping below the horizon, no factor," I continued as if nothing had happened, yet still anxiously waiting for Dave to say something.

"Show me some stalls," he finally volunteered, allowing me to start breathing a bit more easily; it seemed Dave was at least going to wait until the end of this flight before terminating the checkride. In any case, there was no more room for error from now on.

"Hollister traffic, Glider Eight Seven Romeo, maneuvering two miles north at three thousand five hundred feet. Hollister, Glider," I transmitted while visually clearing the area with sweeping turns in both directions. I then performed a stall of moderate depth, recovering from it a tad too quickly, which led to a smaller secondary stall, followed by its own recovery.

Dave then asked for a stall while in a turn. I obliged and entered a coordinated turn with the nose at an unusually high pitch attitude; soon enough, after all the usual warning signs of the stall, the wing started dropping faster, sucking the entire aircraft into an incipient spin. I promptly released the stick forward to allow the nose to pitch back down, applied rudder in the opposite direction of the spin to neutralize the rotation, then picked the nose back up while leaving the wing down in order to resume the original turn.

"Now demonstrate a full stall!" Dave requested. I pulled the stick all the way back, pointing the nose toward the gray layer of clouds up above until nothing else could be seen. Once more, this time in starkly pronounced fashion, Eight Seven Romeo breached, collapsed, and resurfaced like a marine creature.

At Dave's request I then demonstrated 45-degree-bank 360-degree turns in both directions, each time being careful to choose a reference point on the horizon so as to know when to end the turn. And to guarantee that my angle of bank was indeed 45 degrees, I used as visual reference the squares of four screws attaching each instrument to the panel, making sure the horizon was parallel to the imaginary diagonal lines linking pairs of screws from opposite corners. After completing the turns, I noticed that our altitude was getting low, and I told Dave that I was now going to head toward the airport.

On the way back, Dave requested a forward slip, a high-drag configuration that was traditionally used for glide slope control on final approach at a time when gliders were not yet equipped with spoilers. Being comfortable with that maneuver was still important in case the spoilers malfunctioned or were simply not effective enough, as could happen on final approach if still very high or in too strong a tailwind, or even in mid-flight when surrounded by forces of lift so powerful that descending can become a challenge.

I picked a reference point for my heading, then crossed the controls, banking the wings in one direction while yawing the nose in the other. This established a somewhat disorienting yet surprisingly stable configuration that allowed the glider to fly in a straight path while using its own fuselage to create additional drag and increase its rate of sink. As I held that flight configuration, the wind around us was considerably louder, and our seats and spinal columns were at once tilted forward, tilted off to one side, and rotated to the other.

Satisfied with my demonstration of forward slips, Dave asked me to look for lift, quipping that if I could find any in those flat atmospheric conditions I'd be winning the jackpot.

I agreed that it was unlikely we'd find anything that day, and instead addressed his request as a hypothetical task, explaining where and how I would be looking for lift under more favorable conditions.

I said I would first look for visible markers of thermal lift, ideally smooth cumulus clouds with dark flat bottoms, as well as birds or other gliders already circling and climbing. I would also look for ground surfaces most likely to heat up, such as airport runways, parking lots, or dark-colored fields, as well as mountain peaks and mountain sides directly facing the sun or the wind. I also clarified that I would adopt the minimum sink speed (55 mph for our weight) while flying inside of lift, whereas I would shift to the best-glide speed (65 mph for our weight) when flying through sink between areas of lift.

Here again my answer was entirely theoretical and still somewhat coarse and not yet seasoned by experience, seeing as my three months of training, from mid-December to mid-March in dead winter air with no workable lift, had given me the opportunity to glide, but never yet to soar. Reaching the checkride as a soaring virgin was perhaps a bit of an anomaly among student glider pilots, yet one that positioned the act of soaring as a tantalizing reward—one that would probably taste all the better after it had been deservedly earned.

As we approached the pattern entry point, I conducted the landing checklist out loud, taking into consideration the 10-knot surface wind blowing straight down—and therefore clearly favoring—runway 31. I positioned myself for such an approach, and for better stall protection incremented my airspeed by half of the wind speed.

Looking to test my precision, Dave asked where exactly on the runway I was planning to aim, touch down, and stop. I clarified that I would aim my glide slope directly at the large "31" numbers painted on the runway, then after flaring would touch down a bit further beyond these numbers, aiming to completely stop the glider abeam taxiway C ("taxiway Charlie"), the last taxiway before runway 24 intersects runway 31.

After swiftly testing the air brakes, I was glad to find that Dave hadn't decided to pull a trick on me then; he could have either held them shut as I tried to open them, forcing me into a simulated no-spoilers landing involving the use of forwards slips and a much flatter pattern, or he could have held them open as I tried to shut them back, forcing me into a simulated full-spoilers landing involving a much steeper pattern toward the nearest portion of runway I could find.

The presence of wind required making subtle adjustments on each leg of the pattern, lest its rectangular ground track be transformed into a very different polygon. Since I was flying a left pattern and the wind was blowing straight down the runway, I could expect to have a crosswind from the right while on the crosswind leg, a tailwind while flying on the downwind leg, a crosswind from the left while flying on the base leg, and a headwind while on final approach.

To preserve the desired rectangular ground track while flying through the drifting air mass, I had to adjust as follows: on the crosswind leg, I'd establish a heading with a slight crab angle to the right; on the downwind leg, I'd expect to move faster than usual relative to the ground, and with a flatter glide slope that might require opening the spoilers sooner; I'd then make the turn onto base a little closer to the airport than usual; on the base leg, I'd establish a heading with a slight crab angle to the left; on final approach, I'd expect to progress toward the airport more slowly, and with a steeper glide slope that might require using less spoilers; finally, I'd expect to touch down at a lower ground speed than usual, and with the control surfaces remaining responsive longer during the rollout.

I proceeded as planned, being particularly explicit about what I was doing and why, while also regularly calling out my airspeed and making distinct head motions as I kept scanning for traffic.

After a fairly precise landing, I pulled up toward taxiway Charlie and gave one final yank on the spoiler handle; the wheel brake engaged fully and brought the glider to a full stop. Dave contacted Niner Two Zulu on the radio, requesting a "short tow." That we would take off again was the strongest indication yet that my premature release from tow might have been forgiven, but there was no telling what Dave still had up his sleeve.

Seemingly still interested in seeing me succeed, he asked for a smoother takeoff with no unnecessary drift. Reminded of how mediocre my earlier attempt had been even by my own beginner standards, I promised Dave a cleaner takeoff, which I did execute beautifully this second time, imperceptibly detaching Eight Seven Romeo from the runway as if it had done so of its own volition, with no pilot input.

I announced my emergency landing options as we climbed above the remainder of runway 31 and above the first rural fields. To my surprise Dave didn't pull the release below 200 feet for a straight-in landing on 31, nor between 200 and 400 feet for a U-turn landing. We were already 600 feet above ground, an altitude at which a U-turn landing was no longer necessary, and where available landing options were beginning to multiply. "Could you land on runway 24 from here?" Dave asked. I barely glanced toward the runway over my right shoulder before coming back with a confident "yes," and Dave pulled the release. "I want to see a crosswind landing," he explained as the two aircraft parted ways.

I promptly positioned the glider onto an improvised right landing pattern, flying parallel to runway 24 as it lay on my right, and establishing a crab angle to compensate for the crosswind coming from my left. I quickly ran down the landing checklist, and with aviation and navigation both under control, had enough spare cycles to afford the luxury of communication: "Hollister traffic, Glider Eight Seven Romeo, on a right downwind, runway two four. Hollister, Glider."

Before long, I was making a right turn onto the base leg of the pattern. Compressed in my seat and tilted to the right in a 45-degree bank, I unlocked the spoilers and made the last radio call while simultaneously scanning the sky for traffic, monitoring my airspeed indicator, calculating my glide slope, and factoring wind into my trajectory. I was in a state of flow, juggling all aspects of the landing procedure calmly yet alertly.

With a tailwind on the base leg, I initiated the right turn to final early, in anticipation of the crosswind that would be blowing me to the left as soon as the turn began. Once on final, I established what was likely a mix of a crab angle and a forward slip, whatever it took to neutralize the effect of the crosswind and remain aligned with the runway. I flared, touched down, and rolled out while continuing to fly the glider on the ground, keeping the controls crossed to counteract the weathervaning effect of the crosswind.

The glider slowed down gradually, and Dave asked me to stop it. He seemed eager to get out of the cockpit.

We got out of our seats and pushed the glider until it was clear of the runway, past the "hold short" lines painted on the taxiway. Dave remained quiet and unreadable, but I badly wanted to know the outcome of my checkride and didn't have the patience to wait until returning to the office—which it seemed Dave was fully prepared to do—so I asked him directly: "How did I do?"

"Good job!" he replied with sudden enthusiasm, as if this should have been obvious to me. He then offered some guidance on my control inputs, inviting me to think in terms of stick pressure rather than stick motion. With the eloquence of aerial artists and that same sensibility I appreciated in Charlie, Dave observed that while my current inputs did get the job done, I would stand to benefit from "caressing" the controls: continuous, smooth control inputs, he explained, tend to improve safety as they are less likely to create aerodynamic discontinuities that might trigger a stall at airspeeds where stalls should not occur; they also tend to improve performance, especially when working on fragile thermals; finally they tend to improve comfort, an especially important consideration when carrying passengers, who might be prone to airsickness if not merely needing the reassurance of a gentle ride devoid of sudden jolts.

Dave was optimistic that these adjustments in airmanship would come to me naturally as my experience and confidence continued to grow. In the meantime, he recommended that I join the local soaring club, which offered access to state-of-the-art sailplanes that could be flown relatively inexpensively, and that I start working toward obtaining the first of several badges awarded by the Fédération Aéronautique Internationale for attaining various duration, distance, and altitude goals.

Back into the glider operations office, Dave entered some information into an online database, then printed out my temporary airman certificate, informing me that I'd be receiving my permanent certificate from the Federal Aviation Administration within ninety days. We shook hands and said goodbye.

It was official now and I was holding proof in my hands: I was a certificated private glider pilot! Charlie came by to congratulate me, and, just like we had done after my first solo, we walked back to the airfield to commemorate this joint achievement with a photograph of the two of us shaking hands in front of Eight Seven Romeo.

I thought long and hard about why Dave Morss gave me the benefit of the doubt and chose not to fail me for aborting the slack line recovery maneuver. Was it because he wanted to see me succeed after the other examinee had failed? Was it because of some halo effect triggered by my written test results and further reinforced during the interview portion? Was it because he realized that his early comment on the ground maybe did in fact prime me to err on the side of pulling that release rather than not? Was it because of the ambiguous nature of the chain of command during that awkward moment when an examiner takes control of an aircraft of which he is not pilot in command but a mere passenger?

It might have been a bit of all of the above, though I'd like to think it was primarily because Dave determined that my action exhibited the kind of assertive leadership expected of any responsible ship captain; that in the face of a passenger putting the aircraft into a potentially hazardous situation outside of my flight skills envelope, I intervened decisively to put an end to it and restore the safety of the aircraft and its occupants, consistent with my duty as pilot in command.

First Lift

The California grass changed color from green to yellow as fluffy cumulus clouds began to populate the sky. Seasons turned while I took a well-deserved and much-needed eight-week-long break from flying, not only to savor my recent victory, but also, from a safety perspective, because my training schedule for a third triathlon had been ramping up and become so arduous as to leave me constantly too physically tired to also be flying.

I bided my time by attending the monthly meetings of the Bay Area Soaring Associates ("BASA"), the soaring club I was in the process of joining, which allowed me to get acquainted with the sophisticated local culture of cross-country flying while also giving me an opportunity to fly vicariously: the moment I walked into the meeting room, a wall projector was displaying an animation of a glider flying over a terrain model of our region, replicating a club member's recent flight using GPS data collected by an on-board flight recorder. The entire flight trace remained on screen trailing behind the glider, offering me visual proof of the existence of thermals: at once mesmerized and taunted, I watched on as the glider model began circling and climbing into a helicoidal pattern, drawing corkscrew after corkscrew up the virtual sky.

As frustrating as it may have been, staying on the ground while fatigued was absolutely the right thing to do, even though it was arguably the worst time of my budding aviation career to be going on a hiatus; my eventual return, a week after the triathlon, was not only predictably rusty, but also greeted with several variables changing all at once: new instructors, new sailplanes, new procedures, and new weather conditions.

I considered doing a few refresher flights in Eight Seven Romeo before switching over to the fiberglass club gliders, but this approach no longer made sense from a financial perspective: having graduated from my student pilot training, I was no longer allowed to fly Eight Seven Romeo at the discounted hourly rental rates and without taking on significant financial liability risk; in comparison, being a dues-paying member of the local club now afforded me unlimited access to its fleet, and though I still had to pay for the cost of the tows, I could fly club gliders indefinitely with no hourly rental charge while also enjoying the protection of a generous group insurance. And since I was in any case going to be flying the club gliders with instructors until they felt comfortable signing me off to fly them as pilot in command, it made sense to not further delay that inevitable and enviable transition to the club fleet, no matter how abrupt it might be at first.

Club glider N451CH ("One Charlie Hotel") was a magnificent DG-1000S that had once belonged to my instructor Charlie Hayes, after whose birth date and initials it had been named. It was a modern fiberglass sailplane with a maximum glide ratio of about 46:1 (compared to Eight Seven Romeo's 35:1), a retractable landing gear, and, among other bells and whistles, a cushioned interior that had front seat occupants reclining almost horizontally.

I was naturally apprehensive to demonstrate my piloting skills in such a valuable ship, and as I lay down clumsily in the cockpit, waiting for the club's flight committee chairman to hop in the back seat and wondering how I'd be able to fly in this reclining position, I was comforted to find that, resting on the shoulder strap of my parachute, the ladybug had just returned.

Soon enough we were rolling off the ground and up into the air, where I was able to appreciate the superior sound insulation of One Charlie Hotel, as even the aerotow appeared incredibly silent.

We were still flying at low altitude and I had yet to get a good grasp of the controls, when suddenly the glider started buffeting through rocky turbulence. The audible variometer indicating our vertical velocity was chirping frantically, pitching its song up and down like a famous science fiction robot.

"What's happening?" I asked my instructor nervously. Then he told me something I had never heard before: "You're flying in lift! There's lift everywhere!"

A couple of minutes later I pulled the release, which, surprisingly muffled, gently popped like a cork, and at long last I began circling up my very first thermal.

Some pilots never forget the bliss of their first thermal. Others need to wait a bit longer before experiencing the one that for the first time makes them feel like a soaring pilot. My own first thermal, although duly exciting, proved to be less culmination than initiation; as much as the bubbly welcome brimmed with promise as it flung open the gates of heaven, I had yet to earn my proficiency in glass ships and learn how to properly harness lift. Enchantment, therefore, would come later; but I knew then that it would.

First Dance

Reclaiming my flight proficiency in a highly efficient glass ship took work, and after 16 flights scattered over a month of weekends I was finally able to make consistently good landings in One Charlie Hotel and its similar DG-505 companion, N505KM ("Five Kilo Mike"). Nevertheless, this wouldn't earn me the privilege to fly either of them as pilot in command just yet, as the club's flight rules required that I first accumulate a higher number of flights and flight hours in glass ships.

I had the option of doing so either by continuing on with dual flights in the DGs with an instructor or other club member qualified to fly it as pilot in command, or, more independently, more cost-effectively, and with fewer chances of scheduling conflicts, in single-seater SZD-51-1 N106DS ("Six Delta Sierra"), more affectionately referred to as "the Junior," which my instructor had just deemed me ready to start flying.

Without much hesitation I chose the Junior, knowing this would be another frightening but important rite of passage; indeed, flying in a single-seater for the first time in some sense felt like the ultimate first solo, given that I'd be limited to studying the glider on the ground and would not have the luxury of a practice flight with an instructor before flying it on my own.

I spent a long time studying the Junior's manual the night before my first flight, then after a few more dual flights in the DGs the next day, I asked my supervising instructor for some time alone with the Junior and just sat in it for a while on the ground, mentally and physically rehearsing every checklist and flight procedure until all the controls and instruments felt solidly familiar.

The Junior was a cinch to handle on the ground, as it was light enough to be pushed around single-handedly, without the assistance of flight line personnel and golf carts. More importantly, the Junior was a delightful ship to fly. Seasoned club members flying for distance rarely selected it for their cross-country feats due to its relatively poor ability to penetrate headwinds, but for someone more interested in stationary maneuvers close to the home airport like I still was, its low rate of sink and ability to fly nimbly at very low speeds without stalling made it perfectly well-suited for soaring locally and performing tight circles inside the narrowest of thermals.

Even in the absence of lift, the Junior in slow flight would appear to remain completely suspended, hovering in place with barely any noticeable forward or downward motion. And the subtle rainbow tint on its canopy, at times with the daytime moon in the background, added a touch of magic to the contemplative silence of these slow-motion flights punctuated only by the occasional rudder squeak, whose timbre had an underwater quality that sounded a bit ominous at first, but which in time grew to resemble the soothing foghorn of a lighthouse.

The Junior was a glider full of whimsy, and I quickly grew fond of it. The two of us remained exclusive partners throughout the summer, flying a total of 35 flights together, many of them rapid-fire takeoffs and landings in 25-knot wind blowing straight down runway 24.

A west-southwest sea breeze that reliably picked up on most summer afternoons had the unfortunate habit of wiping out most thermals west of the first topographical obstacles it encountered, which weren't for another few miles east of the airport.

On the other hand, because they were barely angled with runway 24 and only carried mild gustiness, these strong and stable headwinds with negligible crosswind components ultimately created very favorable takeoff and landing conditions: steep glide slopes, low ground speeds, short ground rolls, and responsive controls. These helped demonstrate a notion I had only accepted theoretically until then: that takeoffs and landings in strong headwinds, while requiring more awareness and planning, are arguably safer and easier to execute than takeoffs and landings in calm wind.

The benefits were especially noticeable on landing. As long as I was careful to turn onto the base leg sooner than in calm wind to avoid being blown downwind of the airport, the crab angle used on base to neutralize the effect of the crosswind provided a clear view of the airport, along with a head start on the turn to final, which itself felt more like a course correction than a full-fledged turn.

Then once on final, as long as I kept flying the proper approach airspeed without being fooled by the slowness of my forward motion relative to the ground, I'd find myself on a glide slope so steep that it was beginning to look like that of a helicopter. That naturally steep approach allowed me to err on the side of using a bit less spoilers than usual, thereby reducing the rate of descent. Touchdown would then occur with a soft vertical impact and at a low forward ground speed, which, combined with the light weight of the Junior, meant very little kinetic energy to manage during a ground roll that could be as short as a few feet if I engaged the wheel brake quickly.

If anything, the bigger risk was when I actually needed to extend what little energy I had at my disposal in order to keep rolling to the nearest runway exit, as was convenient if this was my last flight of the day, or even critical if another aircraft was landing behind me. I thus learned the value of choosing my aim points judiciously, as these low-energy touchdowns made precision landings a quasi-necessity.

By the end of that windy summer I had accumulated the additional ten hours I needed in glass ships and was ready to return to the DGs, which, after a few more dual flights with an instructor, I got signed off to fly as pilot in command. I began soloing in One Charlie Hotel and Five Kilo Mike, which to my novice pilot senses handled almost exactly the same even though these two aircraft were more like siblings than twins.

What I did notice was how differently they handled from the Junior: their massive wings, to which much of the impressive performance characteristics of the DGs were owed, were broader and heavier and therefore slower and more effortful to roll into a turn. On the flipside, they were also much more stable when traversing wind gustiness, making takeoffs, aerotows, and landings particularly smooth and controlled.

Nevertheless, getting adjusted to these very efficient sailplanes required much caution and much practice: high glide ratios and seemingly perfectly horizontal forward motion may be a blessing at altitude, but when it comes to landing an aircraft that does not want to touch down, preferring to keep floating a few feet above ground on the aerodynamic cushion known as "ground effect" (an effect particularly pronounced for a glider with a 20-meter wingspan), runways suddenly feel very short, and overshooting these elusive targets becomes a real possibility. Glide slope management via judicious use of spoilers became more critical than ever, as was energy management and airspeed control, which had to be maintained within a narrow band: it was no longer sufficient to make sure I was flying fast enough not to stall on final; I now also had to make sure I was flying slowly enough to minimize the length of runway needed to bleed off excess energy during the flare, hold off, and rollout.

And so, just like I had spent the summer familiarizing myself with the Junior, I spent the next few months solidifying my comfort level in the DGs, measuredly exploring their flight envelope while stretching my own limits. Rapid-fire takeoffs and landings were interspersed with longer soaring flights, some of them with me serving as co-pilot to highly experienced club members, whose inspiring example gave me a taste of the boundless potential to fly ever longer, ever further, ever higher, ever more precisely, ever more beautifully, ever more wisely, ever more rewardingly, ever more joyfully. It became clear that, just like Sergei Rachmaninoff once said about music, "[soaring] is enough for a lifetime, but a lifetime is not enough for [soaring]."

These glorious months came on the heels of a significant milestone in my life, and the realization of a fifteen-year-old dream: on May 31, 2011, I officially became a United States Permanent Resident, and with great emotion found my Green Card in the mail a few days later. This resolved more than a decade of uncertainty over the fate of my immigration story, allowing me to sleep more soundly without a Sword of Damocles hovering overhead, as I no longer had to worry about having to pack up all my belongings and leave the country on a moment's notice in the event that I lost my job or felt an urge to quit. It also allowed me to finally give serious consideration to career opportunities outside the limited scope of the specific job function and sponsoring employer listed on the H-1B visa that granted me the conditional right to temporarily remain on American soil.

Of course I was immensely grateful to have journeyed for six years on what I liked to call the U.S.S. Google, a remarkably comfortable and stable aircraft carrier even at the height of the storm that was the recession of 2007-2009, when countless smaller ships were capsizing and hemorrhaging crew members at sea; indeed, unlike droves of less fortunate foreigners who fell victims to a wave of layoffs and were forced to leave the country during that episode, I never truly feared for my job security at Google. That said, comfort and stability were not what I had come to seek in the American West when I first arrived here in 2000, and it was high time for me to hop into my own sailboat and begin searching for new dreams.

I took a trip to Paris to return to my cultural roots, talk to those who had seen me grow up, and take a good look at my life from a 30,000-foot perspective. After much introspection I returned with a list of ideas and avenues to explore, and, with the conviction that I would be leaving the corporate world within a year, I tested the waters with a three-month-long leave of absence; I started taking acting classes to reconnect with my humanistic side, worked my way toward swimming 10 kilometers back-to-back to maintain spiritual altitude, and moved to San Francisco proper to fulfill a promise I had made to myself to live there at some point during my twenties.

My new apartment was located at the intersection of Union Street and Fillmore Street at the heart of the Cow Hollow neighborhood, and overlooked the Golden Gate Bridge, the Palace of Fine Arts, and the rooftops of the Marina district—just the view I had fantasized about for so long. Admittedly, this also meant a northern orientation with hardly any sun exposure in a city already known for fog and cold; and the minuscule one-bedroom apartment, with slanted floors that required special ingenuity when arranging furniture, was in a building old enough to have survived the earthquake of 1906 before serving as a youth hostel in the 1930s. Yet such idiosyncrasies were oddly fitting, injecting character and symbolism to these new beginnings in rougher seas extending toward alluring horizons. I quickly equated my San Francisco apartment to my metaphorical sailboat, finding myself investing considerable amounts of time decorating it and optimizing its interior design, in a way that would make it both comfortable and functional enough for me to proudly call it home—something I had never been able to do ever since my nomadic American adventure first began.

Living in San Francisco meant having to drive twice as far to get to and from Hollister, and having moved to an urban environment from a suburban one added further mental disconnection from the countryside. Yet despite these additional hurdles and the exciting changes taking place in my life (and perhaps aided by the aeronautical charts and commemorative poster prints of my recent aviation milestones now hanging from my bedroom walls),

I somehow managed to remain focused on my soaring challenges. Keeping that thread alive and well, I was even pleased to discover, upon my return from Paris, that my piloting skills were now able to survive an entire month of hiatus without significant decay—at least as long as I continued to regularly practice those skills by means of mental visualization.

Meanwhile, continuing to train new students while monitoring the overall safety of glider operations at Hollister, Charlie was still around. He had remained a benevolent presence on the airfield, a guardian angel often unseen yet ever watchful, vigilantly observing my continued progress from a distance, occasionally jumping in to reveal a blind spot or dispense ever-timely advice. Once in a while the two of us would hop into a DG and fly together again, whenever I felt something about my flying was off and in need of a tune-up, or simply because there was always so much to learn from Charlie.

As autumn deepened, soaring conditions faded and had all but disappeared by the month of December, where just under a year earlier this adventure had first begun. Most of the seasoned pilots, for whom gliding no longer had quite the same appeal as soaring, went into full hibernation mode until springtime and the return of thermals. My own trips to the gliderport also became a bit more sparse, though the good fortune of inexperience kept me motivated to continue flying somewhat regularly, if only to avoid losing my hard-earned and still-fragile proficiency.

I booked One Charlie Hotel one more time before the one-year anniversary of my first glider flight, with the straightforward intention of rounding off this first year with five more pattern tows leading up to my 200th flight. The sky was mostly cloudy, with grey ceilings as low as 3,000 feet that would slowly be rising by another 2,000 feet over the course of the afternoon.

Charlie happened to be available to fly with me that day, so I enlisted his guidance for the first two pattern flights, then, incorporating his feedback, continued on solo while Charlie remained on the ground, acting like an improvised control tower, monitoring the airport's radio frequency and assisting local aircraft with their separation needs. I completed two more uneventful pattern flights, then launched for flight #200.

Releasing from tow above the standard pattern entry point, I turned straight into the crosswind leg. "Hollister traffic, Glider One Charlie Hotel, one mile west, entering left crosswind, runway two four. Hollister, Glider."

The variometer started chirping. Momentary turbulence wasn't uncommon at pattern altitude. This time was different however. The chirping was pitching higher and higher, and wouldn't stop for the entire duration of the crosswind leg. I was gaining altitude, climbing fast, and was debating whether to abort the landing. As if reading my mind, Charlie popped on the radio.

"One Charlie Hotel, Glider Ground."

"One Charlie Hotel."

"One Charlie Hotel, are you in lift?"

"Affirmative. Is it that obvious from down there?"

"Make the most out of it! Climb as high as you can! Fly as long as you can!"

"Copy that, Glider Ground... Hollister traffic, Glider One Charlie Hotel, one mile south, leaving the pattern."

Circling and climbing in strong lift with no other aircraft in sight or on the radio frequency, I exited the pattern vertically. Ascending through that little miracle, I enjoyed even more widespread lift as I neared cloud base. When I got too high, I'd simply dive away from the lift and see if I could find another source somewhere else, and when I got too low having found nothing but flat air or sink, I'd promptly return to known areas of lift. I thus kept playing under the clouds, at a time of year where such frolic tends to be mostly fantasized about, and what had set out as a simple pattern tow was quickly turning into an hour-long soaring flight.

I eventually found my way to the other side of the airport, about a mile north, beneath a larger cloud of a slightly darker shade of grey. I began circling under it, and as I banked my wings into a right turn and looked over my shoulder, it suddenly came to my attention that I was being followed. About a quarter of a circle behind me, tailing One Charlie Hotel at a comfortable distance, at once curious and aloof yet unmistakably at ease: a hawk!

Wings fully deployed and effortlessly holding formation for a while, the majestic bird eventually grew impatient with my inferior thermalling skills and took it upon herself to demonstrate proper form. Tightening her turn, the creature after which One Charlie Hotel and its many predecessors had been modeled passed me on the right and centered her flight path around the core of the thermal. I followed suit, banking my wings more tightly to the right and making further adjustments until our circles matched again, forming a blissful carousel where, diametrically opposed, hawk and glider, biological wonder and engineering marvel, engaged in a dizzying aerial waltz, background revolving in a blur as they circled around each other like binary stars, dancing their way up a double helix twisting into the heavens.

First Guest

Like many joys in life, flying gains in meaning when it is shared with others. As pilots mature in the cockpit and their dependence on responsible others gradually fades away, they may choose to in turn take on responsibility for dependent others. Just as they once progressed from helpless passengers, to docile students, to independent soloists, they may keep on evolving to helpful co-pilots assisting their seniors, reliable mentors guiding their juniors, trusted hosts carrying non-pilots, and consequential instructors influencing the destinies of the next generation of airmen and their respective future passengers.

There was no telling whether I'd personally ever travel to the far end of the responsibility spectrum (a teacher at heart, I certainly couldn't rule it out), but at the very least, the prospect of someday being able to take passengers up for a ride and offer them an experience that until recently most people who ever lived could only yearn for might indeed have been the single most powerful motivator for me to keep improving as a pilot.

I could have legally started taking passengers mere minutes after Dave Morss had handed me my temporary pilot certificate, and then again, with a major cockpit upgrade, as soon as I had been signed off to fly the club's DGs. Yet I felt that anyone willing to trust me with their life deserved better than the minimum requirements, so it was only natural that of all the club privileges I was working toward getting signed off on, the one I most eagerly anticipated and went on to cherish the most would be the "backseat checkout," which authorized club members to fly the DGs from the back seat while yielding the front seat to a passenger, along with its unobstructed panoramic view.

Flying in the back seat was not significantly different from flying in the front seat, but nevertheless required minor procedural tweaks and a brief adjustment period that it was wise to experience with an instructor.

The most obvious hurdle was the passenger's head and headrest straight ahead in the field of vision, an obstruction of varying severity depending on the bulk of their hat and hairstyle, and on how much they moved around.

The other main challenge was a distortion of the visual perspective, caused by the curvature of the front canopy. This effect was felt most acutely during the landing flare, where the ground would appear closer than it really was, luring the novice backseat pilot into an early flare just a couple of feet too high, threatening a hard landing as the glider would stall with no ground to support it.

Another less critical yet possibly more insidious safety consideration was that, while all of the front seat controls were duplicated in the back seat, this was not the case with some of the more miscellaneous instruments, such as the battery switches, the transponder, and the radio knobs. Setting those before takeoff and asking not to touch anything was of course a reasonable precaution, as was carrying a backup handheld radio in the back seat, but it was also prudent to teach passengers how to interact with these basic instrument settings should they accidentally be altered in mid-flight or should a need to alter them arise at any point.

Finally, thanks to some of my prior flights as back seat co-pilot, I was already used to the more upright and cramped configuration of the backseat, and in the process had also discovered the secret consolation prize of back seat flying: that by sitting so much closer to the aircraft's center of gravity, it is easier to feel at one with the glider, and maneuvers can thus be performed more intuitively and precisely.

Shortly after completing my backseat checkout with Charlie and further solidifying my backseat flying proficiency with other club members sitting in the front seat, I received an unexpectedly timely message from my good friend Christopher, who had left Zürich and more recently been living in New York City.

"What are you doing next weekend? Want to go flying?" he asked concisely and tantalizingly, implying that he was embarking on a surprise visit to California.

It was still early March, which meant the weather would be flyable at best and probably not soarable yet, offering a convenient excuse for a flight that would likely turn out to be rather short and basic—the kind that would have been perfect for someone who had never been in a glider before and just wanted a taste. However, since Christopher had already experienced soaring before, a day of booming soaring conditions might have created expectations I could not possibly live up to just yet, and which would have likely left him disappointed as my still limited soaring skills would inevitably be exposed. With our expectations lowered from the onset as they were, we'd at least be able to forget about performance and instead focus on the rewards inherent to simply having this moment in the sky together.

March 10, 2012, the day we settled on, was Christopher's birthday. It was wonderful to hear him want to celebrate the occasion in a sailplane, and truly an honor to have him trust me as his ride pilot. I also found it particularly fitting that he be my very first non-pilot passenger, as I couldn't think of a more appropriate way to thank him for introducing me to the world of sailplanes.

Practically speaking and in the spirit of changing only a few variables at a time, Christopher was also an ideal first passenger, since, not being a first-time passenger himself, he already knew much of what to expect and was rather unlikely to experience any of the adverse reactions I may need to be prepared to handle with some future passengers, such as airsickness, vertigo, claustrophobia, or even panic.

Nevertheless, I prepared intently and aimed to give Christopher the best and safest experience possible. I reserved One Charlie Hotel, the finest aircraft of the fleet, and in the morning conducted three backseat takeoffs and landings in it with an instructor. Then in the early afternoon I completed my first three solo flights in one of the club's two Centrair C101A "Pégase" sailplanes, highly sensitive single-seaters that I'd just been signed off to fly, finally earning full access to all five ships of the club's fleet. By the time Christopher showed up in the middle of the afternoon, I was both in high spirits and fully warmed up, with my skills as sharp as they'd ever been.

True to his character and to a birthday tradition of his, Christopher had spent the previous night exploring nature by himself, this time somewhere around Big Sur, another ninety minutes south along the Central Coast, and I found him taking a nap in his car after what turned out to be a rather tiring adventure in the wild. Luckily he was still ready and eager to fly, so I invited him to my first passenger briefing.

Our first stop was in the back room of the glider operations office, a storage area that the club also used to store its
own equipment. On one of the tables, several brick-sized
batteries, each labeled with the N number of the glider it
belonged to, were quietly charging as red and green diodes
were flashing and blinking. One Charlie Hotel was not re-
presented among them however, as its batteries never needed
to leave the aircraft, where they were constantly recharging
via a solar panel etched into the dorsal part of the fuselage.

Moving right past the chargers, we stopped in front of a
large wall shelf loaded with boxes of maintenance tools,
cleaning supplies, and, of greatest interest to us, a dozen
emergency parachutes piled up in their protective bags. I
looked for my two favorite ones and showed Christopher
how to don his, pointing out that we needed to be careful
not to let the straps dangle freely while near the glider, lest
the swinging metallic buckles turn into wrecking balls that
could dent the fragile fiberglass hull.

I then explained the emergency bailout procedure as it
had been taught to me, for better and for worse only from
hearsay rather than personal experience: "We hopefully
shouldn't have to use these parachutes for anything other
than extra cushioning in our seats today, but in the unlikely
event of an unrecoverable loss of control of the aircraft—as
might result from structural damage or mechanical failure—
we'd have to bail out of the cockpit. You'll most likely
know from our flight configuration that something has
suddenly gone very wrong, and you'll also be hearing me
shout bailout instructions."

"What are they?"

"The exit procedure can be remembered as 'C-B-B:
Canopy. Belts. Butt.' We'll go over this again in context
once you're sitting inside the cockpit, but it doesn't hurt to

start mentally visualizing it now. First, unlatch the *canopy* and push it up and away with your hands. Second, be sure to unstrap your *belts* and not your parachute. Third, get your *butt* out of your seat however you can, using the weight of your head if needed."

"How high must you be for the parachute to open?"

"No lower than 1,000 feet above ground level, but that's when the parachute actually starts opening; exit should begin much higher. Also, once you're out of the sinking ship, the parachute will not open on its own; you'll need to promptly and vigorously pull out the rip cord via that metal handle on the left side of your chest, which should completely detach from the vest and remain in your hand, for you to either keep or discard. Your parachute will then open almost immediately so brace yourself for a tug within the next three seconds."

"Once it's open, can you steer it left and right?"

"You can try, but these emergency parachutes have round canopies and are not nearly as steerable as sports parachutes used by skydivers. Also, be prepared for a steep glide slope and a hard landing; it might help to bend the knees slightly and point the toes down before impact. After touchdown, take off the parachute without delay, unbuckling the chest strap before the leg straps to avoid getting strangled as the wind pulls the canopy away."

With that sobering imagery mostly out of the way, we exited the storage room as I ventured that our thoughts would only be getting more pleasant going forward. Making one last bathroom stop, we proceeded to the airfield entrance, where I punched in the access code and welcomed Christopher through the metal fence, remaining vigilant about taxiing aircraft as I introduced him to the fleet of club sailplanes, and of course dear old Eight Seven Romeo.

Radio in hand, we walked across runway 24 toward the patch of grass where One Charlie Hotel awaited.

In any seating configuration, though especially with a new passenger in the front seat, it is important to conduct a weight and balance calculation prior to the flight; this ensures that the occupied glider will neither be too light nor too heavy, and that the center of gravity will not fall too far forward or too far aft for safe operation. This seldom requires the use of actual scales as the required computation can generally be done in a spreadsheet, inputting the weight of each occupant along with other numerical values obtained from the glider's flight manual and maintenance records. The results indicate how much ballast needs to be included, whether the occupants need to swap seats, and whether the flight is even possible.

Factoring in Christopher's weight and my own, including the additional poundage from our parachutes, I had confirmed the night before our flight that my guest would indeed be able to enjoy the front seat; this came as no surprise given his slender build and barely taller-than-average height, but the calculations mostly helped me determine the specific amount of tail ballast required to keep the glider optimally balanced, which was the very first thing I took care of upon reaching One Charlie Hotel.

The glider had already been flown earlier that same day, but since it had been left unattended for a while, I conducted a thorough preflight inspection from scratch, asking Christopher to kindly stand by quietly so that I wouldn't overlook any important item.

I walked around the glider, examining the hull, the wings, the stabilizers, testing the freedom of motion of the control surfaces and checking the hinges attaching the ailerons to the wings, the rudder to the vertical stabilizer, and the elevator to the horizontal stabilizer. I peered into the pair of static ports on the side of the fuselage, into the pitot tube on the nose, and into the total energy probe on the tail, finding no obstructions. I palpated the tires of the main wheel and tail wheel, and accounted for the wingtip wheels.

Transitioning from the exterior to the interior of the glider, I briefly enlisted my friend's assistance to perform a "positive control check," a critical verification step ensuring full mechanical linkage between the various control surfaces and their respective cockpit controls; I asked Christopher to walk around the glider and stop at each control surface, holding it steady with enough resistance for me to feel at the other end as I moved the corresponding cockpit control along its full range of motion in both directions.

Continuing alone with the inspection of the cockpit, one seat after the other, I verified the taping of the yaw strings, examined the hinges and latches of the canopies and belts, and scanned the seat cushions and the floor for foreign objects or uninvited creatures. I tested the trim and release mechanisms, then, moving on to the instrument panel, adjusted the altimeter, confirmed the zero on the airspeed indicator, flipped on the battery switches, checked the voltage, turned on the audio variometer, set the transponder, and conducted a radio check.

"Thank you for your patience, Chris. I'm ready now. Come on over!" I was excited to continue the passenger briefing and take the time to communicate everything I could to make the flight as safe, pleasant, and collaborative as possible. Luckily my guest was naturally curious and particularly eager to learn the ins and outs of glider flying, which allowed me to indulge in the joy of teaching perhaps a bit more than I otherwise would with someone more interested in enjoying the ride for its own sake.

"The canopy opens on the left side and rotates around the hinges on the right," I began while demonstrating. "This is actually the most fragile mechanism you'll be handling today, so please be gentle when opening and closing it. You'll need to remain mindful about it whenever it is not in its closed and locked configuration, as strong winds or a sudden gust could potentially slam it shut or barge it open. Specifically, never walk away from the cockpit without locking the canopy. Now go ahead and hop in!"

I helped Christopher adjust himself in the front seat, adjusting his belt straps and rudder pedals, then had him close the canopy so we could rehearse the bailout procedure I had outlined in the storage room earlier. With that pessimistic scenario hopefully behind us, I then showed him how to operate the air vents should he desire more fresh air during flight, as well as the small rectangular window cut out into the canopy that could come in handy if he felt like snapping an aerial photograph and wanted a clean shot without any glassy distortions.

Christopher was now eagerly analyzing his compact surroundings, wanting to test his prior knowledge of the various controls and instruments. Reminding him that our two sets of controls were yoked together and moved in unison, I demonstrated the full range of motion of the stick, rudder pedals, and spoiler handle, stressing that whoever is not operating the controls should be mindful to keep these areas clear of obstructions.

"Got it. And what's that other slider below the spoilers?" Christopher asked.

"That's for the retractable landing gear. It's currently in its forward position, meaning the gear is extended. After releasing from tow, we'll pull it back to retract the gear, which will reduce drag and help extend our time aloft."

"I assume you don't want to forget to put the gear back down before landing, right?"

"Yes, landing the glider on its belly would not be good, which is why we use checklists. As a bonus precaution, this glider also has an alarm that goes off if the gear is still up by the time we open the spoilers—which we almost always need to open during the approach."

"Nice. And that trigger on the stick, is that for firing guided missiles?"

"Hah, that's the trim. This particular mechanism happens to be more intuitive than in other gliders I've flown. Whenever you wish to cruise at a certain airspeed, move the stick forward or back until you reach the desired pitch attitude, and then simply pull that trigger to eliminate the resistance needed to hold the stick in that new position. Here, you can give it a try on the ground. Let's say you just climbed into a thermal and want to slow down for a while. Pull the stick back. Do you feel the resistance and how it wants to return to its original forward position? Now keep it held back and pull the trigger. See? No more resistance, unless you try to move it away from that new position."

"Fancy. What about that yellow knob below the instrument panel? Is that the tow release?"

"Yes it is, and you'll be the one pulling it. Also, if at some point you'd like to take over and try to fly the glider yourself, I'll transfer the controls by saying 'your glider' and wait for you to reply 'my glider,' then I'll confirm that 'I'm off.' This simple exchange should prevent the glider from being flown by both of us or neither of us."

As I was crouching by Christopher's side outside the glider, the corner of my eye caught a glimpse of Charlie walking toward us casually. This was a welcome sight as I was eager to introduce the two men who ultimately had the most influence on making that day possible. At the same time, I was also a bit nervous about having my novice briefing come under expert scrutiny in midcourse and this late in the game, at a stage where, when it comes to safety and cool-headed execution, undisturbed self-confidence likely matters more than any last-minute adjustments.

Soon enough Charlie was upon us, quietly positioning himself standing on the other side of Christopher, until our briefing eventually reached a natural pause and I turned to both of them: "Chris, I'd like you to meet Charlie, my primary instructor; he's taught me almost everything I know about flying, and if our flight goes well today it will be largely thanks to him. Charlie, this is my friend Chris, who originally steered me toward gliders and bravely volunteered to be my first passenger today."

After some handshakes and pleasantries Christopher and I returned to our briefing while Charlie listened with interest, at times helping me rephrase a concept more concisely and effectively, the way years of teaching had taught him. The three of us made quite a tableau, representing but one branch of Charlie's pedagogical legacy.

I rounded off the tour of the cockpit with the instruments, pointing out the altimeter, the airspeed indicator, the variometer, the yaw string, and the compass. I helped Christopher recall how to read and interpret each, then added: "Some of the items on your instrument panel are not duplicated on mine in the back seat, so I'll be relying on you to operate them if needed. Let's go over these." After showing him how to use the unduplicated instruments then briefly quizzing him, I hopped in the back seat to rehearse the critical phases of flight and let Christopher know what would be expected of him at each juncture.

I gave him his own miniature takeoff checklist (A-B-C: *Altimeter* set to field elevation of 230 feet, *Belts* secured, and *Canopy* closed and locked), which I'd have him confirm out loud as a subset of my own longer checklist. I also stressed how his cooperation could improve safety: "As the glider starts moving, and for the duration of the tow, please keep your head relatively still or off to just one side of the headrest so I can keep the tow plane in sight at all times. Also, since I'll need my full concentration while we are still close to the ground, let's quietly enjoy the climb and refrain from talking until we reach an altitude of about one thousand feet above ground. The same will apply during the landing approach, but I'll remind you when we reach the pattern entry point."

"How long do you think we'll be up?"

"Since there doesn't seem to be much usable lift today we'll take a fairly high tow to about 4,000 feet above ground. Assuming we find no lift and slowly glide down all the way to pattern altitude at about 1,500 feet above ground, our entire flight should last about half an hour. We can certainly take a second tow afterwards if you're left wanting more."

"Sure, let's see how it goes. Is there anything else I can do to assist you?"

"Yes. Your extra pair of eyes can help make us safer. As much as you can, keep scanning the horizon line for traffic, especially straight ahead, where I have a blind spot. Now, you may be tempted to move your glance in one continuous sweep, but your peripheral vision is actually more likely to detect moving objects if you fixate on a single point of space for a couple of seconds at a time before shifting to another."

"And if I see something?"

"Whenever you spot an aircraft anywhere, please point it out to me immediately even if it doesn't appear to be a risk factor; for instance, if it's straight ahead and clearly above our altitude, you can say 'traffic, twelve o'clock, high,' or if it's over to our right side down below, you can say 'traffic, three o'clock, low.'"

"Will do. Anything else?"

"That should do it. Let's go fly!"

With the exception of self-launching motorgliders, getting a glider up into the air is invariably a synchronized team effort. I started the choreography with a generic radio call: "Glider Ground, Glider One Charlie Hotel is ready for staging. We are on the north side of runway 24." Charlie, who had meanwhile given us some space and gone on to tend to another glider, heard the call and let us know he'd be the one coming to help us taxi. Christopher remained buckled in and I hopped out to walk the wing while Charlie drove the golf cart pulling the glider forward.

The checkered white and orange flag on the golf cart was indicating moderately strong wind favoring runway 24, which the windsock also confirmed. As the glider's main wheel rolled onto the runway centerline, I asked Christopher to pull the release and disconnect from the golf cart, which Charlie rushed off to the side of the runway while the tow plane rolled in. Meanwhile I rotated the glider to face into the direction of takeoff, reintroducing Christopher to that solemn moment where the runway engulfs one's field of vision, its many parallel lines hypnotically converging toward a vanishing point in the distance, locking one's mind into forward-looking focus as takeoff suddenly feels imminent.

I buckled myself in while Charlie removed the tail dolly and hooked us up to the tow plane. Fresh out of our dress rehearsal, Christopher and I completed the takeoff checklist efficiently and confidently, and up we went. Four thousand feet higher, my guest pulled the release and the two aircraft synchronously banked into opposite turns, accelerating away from each other as the ballet formation dissolved.

"Wow," murmured Christopher. "I think that might be my favorite part."

"It's quite a sight, isn't it?"

Christopher had been telling himself that if something were to happen to me in mid-flight, he'd probably still remember enough from his first few instructional flights from a couple of years earlier to be able to land somehow and at least save our lives if not the glider. He was forced to revisit this assumption, however, after I handed him the controls and had to regularly jump back in and return the glider to a safe attitude. Just like Charlie had done for me during my training, I tried breaking things down for Christopher, asking him to focus on one axis of control at a time while I handled the others, all the while pointing out the basic aerodynamic tendencies of the aircraft. But my guest was beginning to feel a bit frazzled and decided to cede back the controls and simply enjoy the ride, conceding: "Hmm, maybe I am at your mercy after all."

He was clearly disappointed that even basic maneuvers appeared harder to perform than he remembered, but he was merely experiencing a sobering reality that I too had been grappling with all along: that accurately assessing the state of one's own flying proficiency after the passage of time is about as challenging as acquiring these flying skills in the first place. In Christopher's defense, a high-performance sailplane like One Charlie Hotel was no training glider, and I too may not have been able to land it safely on my own when I first started flying it; those long, slow-rolling wings were indeed quite powerful and at times unwieldy, and I still had vivid memories of attempted slips inadvertently turning into stall-spins, as well as a few landing flares that had me float over most of the runway, almost overshooting.

My two flights with Christopher, flights #258 and #259, unfolded uneventfully and gracefully. Our initial tow altitude, combined with our glide ratio, allowed us to make some inroads west of the airport, offering us a better view of the Monterey Bay in the distance. Along the way we did stumble upon patches of weak lift that helped us stay aloft and extend our flight another few minutes.

Upon initiating the landing checklist at the end of our second flight, I had Christopher momentarily tune the radio frequency to the airport's Automated Weather Observation System, where I caught reports of near-surface winds as high as 26 knots gusting to 29 knots. Clearly on the high end of my comfort zone, these west-southwest winds were at least conveniently aligned with runway 24.

I calculated the amount of extra airspeed required for stall protection, bumping up our approach speed from 54 to 70 knots, then reminded myself of all the subtle modifications needed to neutralize wind drift in the pattern. I also anticipated a stronger-than-usual "wind gradient," a treacherous weakening in wind strength near the surface that would require us to pitch the nose down further on final in order to maintain our airspeed. Flying at 70 knots was intended to mitigate the consequences of such a wind gradient, but I had to be ready for the possibility that this still may not be sufficient.

Despite all of this planning, what caught me off guard was the late afternoon sun hanging low above the horizon and waiting for us straight down the runway; it greeted us as soon as I was crabbing on base, and I had to land with it in my eyes. There was no need to beat myself up over this however, since I was wearing adequate sunglasses and had limited alternatives anyway; landing on the other runway would have presented a substantial crosswind component that I wasn't sure I could handle, let alone subject a passenger to. Thankfully, my landing was ultimately respectable enough to not warrant any special mention in my flight journal beyond "Landed with sun in eyes."

Over the decade that Christopher and I had known each other, our relationship had become quite nuanced, and I had clearly learned from him as much as he had from me, yet somehow it seemed we both welcomed the occasional opportunity to revisit the mentoring dynamic that had originally brought us close and held a special place in our hearts; this had been one of those days. After returning One Charlie Hotel to its tie-down location, I thanked Christopher for his trust, for allowing me to be his pilot and being the first passenger to take a chance on me. It meant a great deal to me. "Chris, if only you were a girl..." I mused, echoing the playful sentiment he'd express whenever our friendship encountered a high point.

We stopped for burgers on the drive back north, and Christopher shared further impressions: "One thing I realized today is how dramatically different the personality traits of real-life pilots are from what's portrayed in the movies; there's obviously a staggering amount of humility and conscientiousness that goes into this. I used to think you could just schedule a few days of flying lessons, get your license as quickly as possible, and then call yourself a pilot and just fly whenever, whereas after today I think I have a more realistic sense of all the discipline and commitment that takes place behind the scenes."

With his signature blend of idealism and pragmatism, Christopher then turned to more visionary considerations: "Why does aviation have to be that complicated anyway? Some aspects of it remind me of those low-level computer programming languages that keep out all but the most obsessive of engineers, who then come across as wizards for having mastered something unnecessarily arcane, and who with the same amount of effort could have accomplished so much more if only their tools had been more intuitive in the first place. With modern technology and everything we know about elegant design, there has got to be a way to flatten a pilot's learning curve, to abstract out most of the complexity involved, to simplify the user experience and make it much more turnkey and accessible to the masses. Don't you think?"

Faced with such engaging passion I couldn't help but smile enthusiastically, remembering all the times I had heard Christopher brainstorm for solutions to problems big and small, tirelessly advocating for a better world one pain point at a time, addressing each as if the fate of humanity depended on it, because in a way it did. He obviously had a point, and while part of me did relish the ostensible impenetrability of the world of pilots after having paid my own dues, I was well aware that having learned something the hard way was never a good reason for insisting that future generations be precluded from learning it more easily. I applauded my friend's candor as he approached this new field of knowledge with such a healthy questioning attitude, bringing critical thinking, common sense and innovation to a venerable tradition that inevitably sometimes still falls short.

"Aviation could use people like you, Chris. Come back to it sometime."

Back in San Francisco later that evening, I felt inspired to write to Charlie. I had thanked him many times before, but what I had just experienced warranted a more formal expression of gratitude:

Hi Charlie,

Today was a significant day for me. Even though my passenger Christopher had taken a few gliding lessons in the past and knew a little bit about what he was getting into, today was the first time I had the honor of taking a non-pilot up for a ride. I don't think I have ever been entrusted with somebody else's life before, at least not to such an extent, and I want to thank you for everything you have done to help me reach this important milestone in my journey as a glider pilot. I still have much to learn and the road ahead remains fraught with dangers, but I wanted to take a moment to share with you the great joy I was able to experience today, and the new meaning it gave to all the character-building hard work of the past fifteen months, much of it under your auspicious guidance. Sharing the delights of soaring is a gift for both the pilot in command in the back seat and their front seat passengers, and I have great admiration for what you as a flight instructor have chosen to do as a career, and for the benevolent way with which you do so. Thank you Charlie, and I look forward to flying with you again soon.

Joe

Charlie wrote back the following morning:

Joe,

Thank you for your kind words, and congratulations on reaching this milestone. I don't know that I can accurately convey the sense of satisfaction I feel after reading your message but you did me good. I was impressed by the thorough and enthusiastic briefing you provided your passenger. I have admired the diligence and dedication you have put forth in acquiring your license as well as adding to your gliding resume with BASA. You deserve to be proud!

Regards,

Charlie

First Rescue

Thirty nautical miles east-southeast of Hollister Municipal Airport, and with its own share of danger and poetry, Panoche Valley and its undisclosed airstrip is to aspiring cross-country glider pilots flying out of Hollister what the Moon is to interstellar space explorers: a proof of concept, a first challenge, a stepping stone on the way to ever more distant objectives. It is situated far enough from Hollister that on an average soaring day it can only be reached by gliding out of the inverted cone of space wherein Hollister remains within glide range; yet it is also close enough that the odds of being able to later return to that cone and land back home are still favorable.

Airport hopping, or seamlessly transitioning from the safe glide cone of one airport to that of the next, constitutes the basis of disciplined, responsible, and safe cross-country soaring. Venturing into Panoche Valley trains the mind to become comfortable with that very paradigm, as it forces one to decisively leave the home airport behind and commit to treating the airstrip away from home as if it were the intended home destination. While it may not be the preferred landing site, it may well be the safest one within glide range, and sooner or later, being fully prepared to land there will inevitably materialize into actually having to land there.

Flight #288. September 3rd, 2012. (The world had just lost, on August 25, iconic glider pilot Neil Armstrong, of Apollo 11 fame. This flight is dedicated to him, and to the values he represents.)

"Five Kilo Mike, do you copy?" It was Charlie.

I replied with my position and altitude, as was customary for such routine calls between two gliders in mid-flight: "Five Kilo Mike is three miles west of Panoche at three thousand five hundred feet."

Except this was no routine radio call. "Five Kilo Mike, this is Eight Seven Romeo on the ground at Panoche. We need your help..."

A crater-like area of low flat terrain nested in the Diablo Range, carpeted with golden grass prairies stretching all the way to the encasing hills, and entirely disconnected from civilization except for a lonely country road traversing it, Panoche Valley offered a precursory hint of the otherworldly desolation that characterized the high desert plateaus of the American Southwest. Known for hosting bird species of special interest, and named after a coarse type of sugar once harvested locally by native Indians, the lunar valley harbored so few artificial landmarks that it was able to lend its name to almost every one of them without redundancy.

Scattered across Panoche Valley were the cattle fields and rural structures of the unincorporated village community of Panoche, connected to the outside world through each of the three vertices of the roughly triangular valley; nestled against the southern base of the triangle, Panoche Road provided exits to the east and west, and, perpendicular to it and marking the height of the triangle, Little Panoche Road wandered north around the Panoche Hills with the primary purpose of providing access to the tranquil health resort of Mercey Hot Springs. At the south center of Panoche Valley, just west of the inverted T intersection where Panoche Road branched into Little Panoche Road, the Panoche Inn, a rustic bar and restaurant primarily frequented by motorcycle enthusiasts, sat on the south side of the road. Just north of it across the road, at an elevation of 1,340 feet, lay a parcel of land enclosing a barely noticeable grass airstrip not listed on aeronautical charts, and which the soaring community playfully referred to as "Panoche International Airport," or more simply just "Panoche."

Except for the once- or twice-annual weekend when pilots from Hollister and other Northern California gliderports would gather inside Panoche Valley and turn Panoche International Airport into a bustling center of glider launch operations (complete with a barbeque dinner catered by the Panoche Inn), there were usually no good reasons to choose Panoche as a deliberate flight destination, and the lonesome airstrip mostly served as a backup landout option when gliding back to the home airport proved infeasible.

Deliberate care was taken to mow the grass and fill up gopher holes at the beginning of each soaring season, making the Panoche airstrip generally safe enough not only for a glider to land on but also for a tow plane to land on and then depart from with a glider in tow. This allowed stranded pilots to opt for an "aero-retrieve" instead of the less expensive but more time-consuming ground retrieve typical of most off-field landings (in which case the glider is disassembled and loaded in pieces into a ground trailer driven by a tow vehicle from and back to the home airport, where the glider is eventually reassembled).

"Five Kilo Mike, this is Eight Seven Romeo on the ground at Panoche. We need your help contacting Hollister Ground to request an aero-retrieve. There is no cell phone reception down here, the Panoche Inn is closed today, and we're too low behind the mountains separating us from Hollister to establish radio contact with anyone on the other side. You might be our only communication link with the outside world. Could you please relay a message for us on the Hollister radio frequency?"

"Copy that, Eight Seven Romeo. Go ahead."

Earlier that afternoon, I had merrily glided Five Kilo Mike east toward the hills just north of the western vertex of Panoche Valley, finding sturdy thermals above the usual mountain peaks despite an above-average amount of haze that reduced visibility in the distance. Shortly thereafter, Eight Seven Romeo, flown by Charlie and one of his students, joined me in the valley, which we had entirely to ourselves. It was Labor Day, and the sky was surprisingly empty for a national holiday, perhaps because it was a Monday and many pilots had already gone flying earlier during the long weekend.

Collaborating together, our two gliders doubled the efficiency of our search for usable lift. Each aircraft behaved as an auxiliary variometer to the other, measuring the vertical velocity of the air mass remotely and broadcasting the results by the sheer act of climbing or sinking. Further facilitating our search, we had switched to a more private radio frequency where we could regularly communicate without overwhelming distant aircraft with information that bore no relevance to them.

Each of us at various points managed to climb close to 10,000 feet of altitude, consistently with the limits predicted in the soaring weather forecasts for the day. As I reached the top of the atmospheric boundary layer, I even briefly climbed into a qualitatively different upper air mass where visibility suddenly burst to infinity as immaculate blueness filled my sight, and from which vantage point the haze of the lower air mass could be seen accumulating increasingly densely against the horizon. As I looked straight down through several thousand feet of haze, the ground, while still visible, had become noticeably more faint, and as I descended back from clarity to relative murkiness, Panoche Valley took on a more ghostlike appearance.

By restricting sunlight, haze was reducing the strength of thermals, and while this phenomenon hadn't seemed to have any measurable effect until then, the curse eventually materialized. As our two gliders progressed further east above the hills south of Panoche Valley, we both got caught in widespread heavy sink and, forced to retrace our steps through even more sink, quickly lost most of our precious altitude. Eight Seven Romeo, with its higher sink rate and lower glide ratio, had paid a steeper price and was on the ground in no time; and Five Kilo Mike, while still airborne three miles west of Panoche at 3,500 feet of altitude (and a mere 2,160 feet above the landing field elevation), was barely scraping for lift at the edge of its safe glide cone.

"Eight Seven Romeo, Five Kilo Mike. I switched over to the Hollister frequency and attempted to relay your message a few times, but received no reply. I'm probably too low as well, and have only been getting lower. I need to concentrate on climbing for a while and will make further attempts to contact Hollister traffic if I can get higher. Please stand by."

"Copy that, Five Kilo Mike. Standing by. Thank you, and good luck!"

It was Charlie who had first revealed to me the existence of Panoche, when in preparation for my checkride he borrowed my sectional aeronautical chart to mark it with the location of the unpublished airstrip, drawing a small circle with a horizontal line across it to represent the roughly east-west orientation of the lone runway. Ruler and compass in hand, I had then drawn a set of concentric circles around Panoche, Hollister, and other nearby airports to delineate their respective safe glide cones; these estimated the minimum altitudes required at any given point in space, assuming calm wind and taking into account the maximum glide ratio of Eight Seven Romeo reduced by a safety coefficient adjusted to reflect my limited experience.

It had been a long time since Dave Morss and I used that annotated map to discuss a hypothetical cross-country flight from Hollister to Panoche, and I had since redrawn, on a fresh map, more widely-spaced glide circles that reflected the flatter glide cones afforded by the higher glide ratios of Five Kilo Mike and its club fleet companions. Panoche was certainly more accessible in Five Kilo Mike than it would have been in Eight Seven Romeo, and the odds of making it back to Hollister were also higher as less altitude was needed to initiate the final glide home. Furthermore, with its lower sink rate and overall superior flight characteristics, Five Kilo Mike was more likely to keep climbing in borderline soaring conditions that would cause Eight Seven Romeo to sink.

Such considerations did not however take pilot skill into account, and it was unclear whether Five Kilo Mike flown by a novice like myself really was less likely to land at Panoche than Eight Seven Romeo flown by a seasoned pilot like Charlie. All things considered, if Charlie had been forced to land at Panoche, there was a very good chance I might be joining him on the ground before long.

I was circling through choppy lift, periodically glancing at the altimeter: 3,500... 3,400... 3,500... 3,400... 3,500... 3,600! "Any traffic near Hollister, Glider Five Kilo Mike, does anyone copy? ..."

No reply. 3,500... 3,400... 3,500... 3,400... 3,300... 3,200...

The situation was getting dire. If I was unable to climb back up high enough to relay Eight Seven Romeo's message, I would eventually be forced to join Charlie and his student on the ground at Panoche, and the three of us would find ourselves stranded in the middle of an abandoned valley with no communication link to civilization whatsoever. We'd have to spend the rest of the afternoon in the desert heat, with limited water supplies and the best shade in miles found right under the wings of our aircraft.

Keeping an eye on the ground for rattlesnakes, we'd have to take turns monitoring the untied gliders vulnerable to wind gusts, scanning the sky for any overflying traffic while issuing periodic radio calls, and standing by the side of Panoche Road hoping to stop the rare ground vehicle and convince the driver to make a phone call for us a few miles later as cell phone reception returned. If none of this proved successful we'd then have to walk several miles toward the closest isolated barns, hoping not to be greeted as trespassers.

Hopefully, at some point in the late afternoon, Hollister Soaring Center would attempt to contact us on the radio and fail to hear back, eventually starting to worry about our status and possibly dispatching an airplane toward Panoche. There was, however, no guarantee that this would happen early enough in the day to allow time for two separate aero-retrieves, both of which would have to be completed before sunset while our gliders were still legally allowed to fly. If there was only time for one aero-retrieve, we'd likely be spending the entire evening painstakingly conducting a ground retrieve in the dark for the second glider. And if for whatever reason Hollister somehow failed to look for us, spending the night in Panoche Valley, underprepared as we were, promised to be a memorable adventure, albeit unpleasant if not outright hazardous.

The altimeter indicated 3,200 feet of altitude above sea level, but I was a mere 1,860 feet above the Panoche airstrip, and even more uncomfortably close to the ground as I hovered over the first hills surrounding Panoche Valley. Already too low to reach the most reliable and powerful thermals located above the higher peaks, I was desperately clinging to terrain apt to generate better lift than the flatter valley below. I slowly explored my way from one hill to the next, inching toward those closest to the airstrip, just south of it, where I'd have more room to keep searching for lift at low altitudes without constantly worrying about falling below the safe glide cone.

Nevertheless, I was unmistakably running out of options and could no longer afford to reject thermals that would have been deemed too weak to bother stopping for at higher altitude. I was circling almost constantly, often through thermals so narrow that I'd be flying half of a circle in lift and the other half in sink, with the variometer swinging erratically from barely positive to barely negative, averaging zero sink as the altimeter hardly budged, except occasionally downward.

More discouraging were the déjà-vus, as I descended below each altitude mark not just once, but multiple times in a matter of minutes, briefly reclaiming some of the lost altitude only to lose it again, and again. I became acquainted with soaring defeat, realizing that the process leading up to a landout decision was no sudden surrender, but a growing anguish accompanied by a sinking feeling, sensorial and psychological, a steady decline interspersed with momentary hope dashed by further disappointment, not unlike the distressing loss experienced while witnessing the value of a financial asset cascade into worthlessness.

My back was against the wall. Charlie and his student had been on the ground for at least half an hour, and somehow I still hadn't given up on staying airborne. Maneuvering defensively and hoarding altitude, I was tweaking my circles gently, mainly once per revolution, carefully sensing what was happening at any given instant while deliberating on the nature and timing of my next input. Smaller micro-adjustments were also taking place more continuously, according to a more intuitive moment-to-moment feedback loop that time spent aloft inside the forces of nature had begun to shape over the past several months. One recent week in particular had been instrumental in equipping me with the soaring skills and tenacity necessary to hang on.

I had begun that summer by trailering the disassembled Junior across the Sierras, to the weeklong "Thermal Camp" intensive training course offered in Nevada at the Air Sailing gliderport, a self-powered desert oasis entirely dedicated to the pursuit of soaring and blessed with exceptional weather conditions that offered a variety of challenges ideally suited for expanding one's skills envelope.

The nights, which I imagined spectacularly starry when the moon wasn't shining, were spent in sleeping bags inside rudimentary rental trailers while arid temperatures dropped to their cold extreme and the howls of the wind progressively yielded to those of coyotes.

The mornings, inaugurated with a much welcome warm shower, were spent more comfortably in well-maintained facilities clustered around the air-conditioned clubhouse, where camp participants, mentors, and instructors would all gather around a table, a whiteboard and a projector for a full morning of classroom instruction.

At noon, eager to put our newfound knowledge to practice, we would don oxygen cannulas and take off from a field elevation of 4,300 feet, where the high-altitude air was made even thinner by hot temperatures, resulting in longer takeoff rolls, higher ground speeds before lift-off, higher true airspeeds once airborne, and flatter climbs.

The tows were bumpy and chaotic enough to be reminiscent of my very first instructional flights, except this time the turbulence was genuinely exogenous, resulting from wind gusts and thermals powerful enough to momentarily twist the tow rope into a mild helicoid, spontaneously introduce alarmingly large slack in the rope (of the kind Dave Morss had attempted to artificially create during the checkride), or even bump the two aircraft one after the other up a markedly tall step. We'd also find ourselves thermalling while on tow, as the tow planes would attempt to optimize fuel consumption and compensate for lower-than-usual climb rates by deliberately seeking out thermals and banking tightly to remain inside of them. Releasing from tow offered only temporary relief as violent turbulence would eventually return in free flight without warning, sending water bottles and handheld radios flying out of their side pockets and threatening to cause improperly harnessed pilots to hit their head against the canopy.

During one such bumpy episode, as I was circling while determining where to go next, I glimpsed about four or five other gliders thermalling at the same altitude clustered together in a narrow slice of the horizon. "I am not going in there," I instinctively decided, heading instead for a less promising area that had the virtue of being unoccupied. Mere minutes later I was prey to a whole new bout of turbulence that required my full attention, and I had been oblivious to the recent commotion on the radio, until I perked up at the chilling word "mid-air." Did two of the gliders I just avoided end up crashing into one another?

Mid-air collisions are unforgiving accidents that are often fatal, and there was nothing helpful I could do from up there except be thankful for my own safety and continue to control my own ship while remaining calm and vigilant. "Fly the glider, fly the glider," I told myself with a voice that was beginning to sound less like Charlie's and more like my own. I was being jerked around in heart-stopping turbulence just above the red rocks east of the gliderport, fearing the dreaded low-altitude stall and barely making any altitude gains. Whenever I managed to hoist myself up above the nearby ridgeline, the emerald splendor of Pyramid Lake would momentarily appear in the background, only to disappear again as I floundered back lower. And if the horrific news of the mid-air collision, while emotionally charged, bore no immediate relevance to my own present challenging situation, neither did the subsequent updates that revealed that the two pilots involved in the crash had miraculously both been able to land their damaged gliders safely.

Such was one of many notions that, through the test of experience, took on deeper meaning for me at Air Sailing: that a pilot in command must continue to fly his ship with composure even when disaster strikes nearby; and if himself in dire straits, then as long as his ship remains flyable.

I cracked through 4,000 feet above Panoche Valley, and the radio crackled for a brief second, until the pregnant pause yielded to a crisp energetic voice:

"Glider Five Kilo Mike, Skyhawk Seven Echo Sierra fifteen miles southeast of Hollister, I can hear you loud and clear. Go ahead."

"Seven Echo Sierra, could you please relay to Hollister Ground that the gliders at Panoche are requesting a tow plane for an aero-retrieve?"

"Understand gliders at Panoche are requesting that Hollister Ground dispatch a tow plane for an aero-retrieve. I will attempt to relay."

"Thank you. Standing by..."

"Glider Five Kilo Mike, Skyhawk Seven Echo Sierra."

"Seven Echo Sierra, go ahead."

"Good news. Hollister Ground received your message and will be dispatching tow plane Niner Two Zulu toward Panoche. ETA forty minutes."

"Wonderful. Thank you so much!"

"Glad I could help. Good luck with the aero-retrieve!"

I eagerly switched back to the radio frequency where Charlie was waiting.

"Eight Seven Romeo. Five Kilo Mike."

"Five Kilo Mike, go ahead."

"I was finally able to relay our message, and Niner Two Zulu should be here in about forty minutes."

"That's great news, Five Kilo Mike. Thank you!"

"You're welcome. I'll try to stay up and keep climbing."

Soaring conditions had not improved however, and I gradually lost all the altitude I had painstakingly acquired; so much so that, by the time Niner Two Zulu entered Panoche Valley and announced its intention to land, I had already extended my landing gear. Exercising my right-of-way, I called the tow plane to claim the airstrip.

"Niner Two Zulu, Five Kilo Mike. Please be advised, I'm getting low and will likely be landing before you. I'm just about to reach the pattern entry point."

"Copy that, Five Kilo Mike. Go right ahead. I'm still a couple minutes away and can extend further if needed. I'll look out for you."

I had just initiated the turn into the pattern, when powerful energy suddenly lifted the glider. I kept the wings banked for one whole circle, during which the variometer remained solidly in positive territory. Several revolutions later, the altimeter was still steadily rising, at which point I retracted the landing gear and aborted the landing.

"Niner Two Zulu, I'm just above the pattern entry point in strong steady lift and climbing. Will attempt to work this thermal for a while. You are clear to land first."

"Copy that, Five Kilo Mike. Inbound for landing. I have you in sight."

By the time the thermal topped out a few minutes later, I had gained enough altitude to make a dash for the high terrain just west of Panoche Valley, where with enough luck I might catch one more strong thermal and get high enough to glide back to Hollister. As I made my way toward the hills, the tow plane landed at Panoche, but then instead of performing the aero-retrieve right away, Charlie and his student decided to complete a "Panoche checkout," a set of takeoffs and landings that allows an instructor to confidently endorse a pilot to use the Panoche airstrip.

As I found out a year earlier during my own Panoche checkout, taking off from Panoche can be tricky indeed: the tow plane tends to raise a thick cloud of dust into which even the tow rope vanishes, and great care must be taken to keep the glider laterally centered and wings level, lest a wing get caught in the nearby sagebrush and the glider be yawed into a ground loop. I had read about this type of hazards, but didn't realize how unforgivingly quickly they tend to unfold in practice. I was therefore fortunate to experience an incipient ground loop during my Panoche checkout, with an instructor who knew to immediately pull the release and just as promptly apply the wheel brake. This fortuitous demonstration reinforced the importance of mentally rehearsing the abort procedure before every single takeoff, knowing exactly where to reach out for the release knob and the brake handle, and keeping the left hand close to these controls during the takeoff.

The hills west of Panoche were supposed to host what local glider pilots called an "elevator"; that is, terrain that generates fairly reliable lift. The sweet spot's exact location varied of course, depending on a few predictive weather factors along with the chaotic whims of nature. I searched those hills in vain, finding only what perhaps would have been the elevator in less borderline soaring conditions, and ultimately finding myself forced to retreat into the valley and toward the Panoche airstrip yet again.

The afternoon was wearing on and I had already been flying for about four hours. What had started as a brief excursion was shaping up into my longest solo flight to date. More worrisome was that I'd never operated the controls continuously for so long before. The flight was becoming uncomfortable; I just wanted to land, stand up, stretch, relieve myself, and mostly take a break from the relentless concentration effort that was fast depleting my resources and making me less safe with every passing minute.

I knew I had to get out of Panoche Valley soon or concede defeat and land at Panoche. The problem with that second scenario was that my own aero-retrieve might not be guaranteed, considering that evening was approaching and the merry trio was still doing takeoffs and landings. Not only was the first aero-retrieve not yet under way, but the impromptu pattern tows at Panoche had used up enough of the tow plane's fuel that, instead of simply towing Eight Seven Romeo to the halfway point between Panoche and Hollister and then turning around to fetch Five Kilo Mike, the two plane would now need to fly all the way back to Hollister, refuel, and then fly all the way back to Panoche. It seemed everyone had assumed I was assuredly going to succeed at working my way home without an aero-retrieve.

Not wanting to experience the irony of finding myself stranded at Panoche after having made the aero-retrieve possible in the first place, and regretting the proverbial notion that no good deed ever goes unpunished, I managed to draw out of the depths of necessity one last surge of willpower.

Slightly west of the airstrip I lucked into a thermal just as strong as the one I'd found earlier when aborting the landing. Propelled to higher altitude, I made sure to truly climb as high as I could before heading west for my final attempt at finding and riding the elusive elevator. Meanwhile on the ground, Eight Seven Romeo was finally getting hooked up to Niner Two Zulu for its long-anticipated aero-retrieve, and the radio chatter between the two aircraft provided welcome background noise in an otherwise increasingly lonely valley. The late-afternoon September sun was getting low and mountain shadows were lengthening. Thermals were growing weaker, yet at the same time wider and more consistent, which perhaps explains why, just southeast of the highest peak of the elevator area, I stumbled at long last into lift wide enough for the better part of a full circle.

Conjuring everything I knew about the subtle art of soaring, and determined not to lose that tenuous column of rising air, I made only careful, incremental adjustments while keeping my circles tight. The variometer occasionally dropped into negative territory, but the average climb rate remained positive. My spirits were slowly becoming more hopeful as I surpassed the 6,000-foot mark for the first time since Eight Seven Romeo had been forced to land. If only I could climb to 7,000 feet before that thermal expired!

Gaining enough altitude to escape over the mountains, the engine-powered tow formation flew one large circle above Panoche Valley then started heading west-northwest toward Hollister. The tandem passed me at my altitude just a few hundred feet away, briefly eclipsing the sun as it continued to climb.

"Five Kilo Mike, we're flying through some pretty good lift right here!" Charlie reported helpfully.

"Copy that. I'm in decent lift myself, but I'll keep that spot in mind. Thanks!"

"Alright, hang in there; you're almost high enough! We'll be staying in touch over the radio."

Sliding away from the sun, the two dark silhouettes regained their bright colors, and with a mix of envy and satisfaction I watched the starred-and-striped glider and its red-tailed rescuer disappear into the evening haze.

Left behind in Panoche Valley and alone in my struggle, I continued circling. 6,100... 6,200... 6,300... Each hundred feet was taking longer to climb. The thermal, weak to begin with, was weakening further with height, and at any time could top out or even stop working altogether. 6,400... 6,500... I glanced longingly toward the horizon, where, behind several ridges fading into haze, Santa Ana Peak stood above the skyline in the direction of Hollister. 6,600... 6,650... 6,675...

I was barely climbing any more, and the inner bargaining began. How much altitude did I really need? Surely the 7,000-foot glide circle I'd drawn on my sectional chart was a conservative guideline that could be slightly disobeyed... but by how much? Then again, what if I were to hit heavy sink or strong headwinds on the way back? Wouldn't that conservative estimate turn out to be an aggressive one after all? And if I were to get low, would I be able to locate the closest airport in time and then confidently land there even though I'd never done so before? 6,700... Should I just go now? Ever the mind-reader, Charlie weighed in before I'd even think of asking.

"Five Kilo Mike, what is your position and altitude?"

"Five Kilo Mike is still circling over the same spot at six thousand seven hundred."

"Alright, you're high enough! The air is perfectly still on the way back and the headwinds are light, so in this glider you easily have Hollister in glide. Come on home!"

"Roger that. Five Kilo Mike heading toward Hollister!"

I pointed the nose toward Santa Ana Peak and leveled the wings, all at once exiting the turn, the thermal, and the forsaken valley. Within moments all turbulence faded away and the air became glassy smooth, variometer sitting still just below the zero-sink mark. I pitched and trimmed Five Kilo Mike to its best-glide speed, settling into a lulling cruise mode for the final glide home.

Traversing ridge after ridge, I gradually made my way across miles of hilly terrain harboring scant emergency landing options, which, along with other neighboring landmarks, I had mainly studied on satellite imagery and was still learning to reliably identify from the cockpit. Immersed in a steady wind soundscape perturbed only by the occasional banking necessary to glance at the ground immediately below, I eventually reached "Release Ranch," recognizable by the conspicuously neat row of planted trees lining its access road, above which I had released from tow a few hours earlier. Release Ranch was almost at the halfway point of the glide home, and I still had a full 6,000 feet of altitude.

Breathing more easily by the minute, I passed the remaining landmarks one by one: first the mansion and airstrip of NASA director and notable glider pilot Paul Bikle (who in the 1960s set long-standing soaring world records), then the Tres Pinos area and its skydiving drop zone, followed by the plateau's eventual drop-off into flat terrain that forked around Santa Ana Peak into Quien Sabe Valley on the right and Santa Clara Valley on the left (the latter once known as "The Valley of Heart's Delight" due to its sense-pleasing abundance of fruit orchards and flowering trees).

I flew to the left of Santa Ana Peak, shortly thereafter passing by the slightly shorter Henrietta Peak and its radio towers site, above which sometimes rose a powerful thermal that soaring pilots could fuel up on toward the beginning of a flight out of Hollister. At the foot of Henrietta Peak lay Christensen Ranch Airport, which offered a backup landing option in the event of a glide home falling just a couple of miles short. I wouldn't have to land at Christensen this time however, as I finally reached the home airport with plenty of spare altitude.

I glanced at my wristwatch and decided to extend my flight just a few more minutes, hoping to reach the five-hour mark. Raising the glider's nose slightly, I slowed and trimmed to minimum sink speed, overflying the airport upwind to the west. I settled into mild lift produced by the sea breeze converging with the continental air mass and having nowhere to go but up. Facing the Monterey Bay and the Pacific Ocean with the low sun in my eyes, I took a moment to reminisce about a breathtakingly poetic flight I shared with Charlie on that same western heading less than a week earlier, logging my 100th flight hour in atmospheric conditions unique enough around Hollister for even Charlie to describe the experience as "magical."

It was a day where advection fog had formed above the ocean and become a well-defined, unbroken layer of low stratus clouds stretching infinitely far above the water while hardly covering any land. Meanwhile, a powerful sea breeze was blowing inland at around 20 knots, slowly pulling the cloud layer along with it while also being deflected up and down into mild oscillating waves wherever it collided with a mountain ridge.

We had taken a 3,000-foot tow then slowly doubled our height above the ground as Charlie showed me how to patiently harvest the subtle but consistent and pervasive wave lift. Having recently returned from Air Sailing and its rambunctious thermal lift, I would have easily overlooked this finer type of lift on my own, mistakenly dismissing it as too weak to be worth stopping for, if I ever noticed it in the first place. I once again came to appreciate why others jested that Charlie had a special ability to smell lift. The finesse required at the controls took some time to adjust to and revealed a qualitatively different facet of the art of soaring, one that seemed accessible only to those pilots who could calm their mind and truly listen to what the glider was whispering into their ear. It was in that quasi-meditative state that Charlie and I continued climbing and progressing further west.

With almost 6,000 feet of altitude in reserve and our being upwind of the airport in a strong wind that would stretch our glide home, we were able to safely venture surprisingly close to the ocean, right up to and even above the semi-infinite cloud layer, until it filled our field of vision. From this perspective it appeared that the white cotton blanket wasn't cloaking just half the earth below us, but all of it. Spectacular in its own right, that ostensibly panoramic cloudscape was all the more extraordinary because it was a forbidden sight. Woe to those glider pilots who get themselves trapped above an unbroken cloud layer with no engine to escape toward clearer sky and without the instruments required to safely descend through the visual barrier while preserving their sense of orientation and remaining clear of obstacles. Thankfully our own vantage point was a safe one, and our entrapment a mere illusion.

A simple look down confirmed this, revealing that while the clouds moved inland as fast as the air mass that carried them, they were like a conveyor belt continuing to exist while disappearing from sight at the conveyor's end: the fast-moving clouds were vaporizing as soon as they reached the end of the layer, which itself was moving inland only slowly if at all. Watching these substantial clouds vanish almost instantaneously was mesmerizing. So too were the moments immediately preceding their disappearing act, where, like water flowing through the immutable shape of river rapids, they gracefully undulated up and down wave crests and troughs that themselves remained stationary. Meanwhile, parallel to the nearby mountain ridge and just downwind of it, a roughly cylindrical and slightly tentacular rotor cloud slowly twisting around its axis completed the spellbinding tableau.

My wristwatch confirmed that I'd been airborne for over five hours; it was time to return from my reverie and finally land. Mindful of the evening sun shining straight down runway 24, I selected runway 31, safely handling the 10-knot crosswind before touching down and rolling out in quiet triumph.

Stopping abeam taxiway Charlie where just over one hundred flight hours ago this parallel thread of my life had all started, I felt a gratitude that results not from any one particular flight, but from the totality of the experience of being a glider pilot, of practicing the art of soaring as an affirmation of life; past adventures, present privilege, and future possibilities, danger and poetry, freedom and responsibility, solitude and engagement, all combined into the transcendent joy of being an aeronautical explorer. To seek and discover new wonders, new perspectives, new inspirations, and to return to earth with an elevated sense of purpose and an eagerness to share those treasures with the world; this, in whatever small and fleeting way, is now my role, my participation, in the burgeoning, vulnerable, limitless destiny of human flight.

Epilogue

As of this book's publication in 2016, Joe Karam and Charlie Hayes are still soaring across the sky of California, although both have relocated in separate directions outside of the San Francisco Bay Area.

Joe moved south to pursue artistic endeavors in West Hollywood, and now primarily flies at Southern California Soaring Academy's Crystal Airport (46CN) at the edge of the Mojave Desert.

Charlie moved north to Williams, where he continues to teach as a flight instructor at Williams Soaring Center's Williams Gliderport (CN12) in the Sacramento Valley.

Christopher Pedregal still resides in New York City, where he is spearheading an internet venture in the field of education. He recently married in the French countryside, with Joe presiding over the ceremony.

To contact the author, please e-mail
joekaram@dangerandpoetry.com

Acknowledgments

Special thanks to the readers of a preliminary draft of this manuscript, whose honest and thorough feedback has been invaluable in arriving at the present version: **Dale Masters**, **Max Sokoloff**, **Charles Feng**, **Ayelette Robinson**, and **Salvo Lavis**. Thanks also to **Vivien Nirascou** and **Tobias Deml** for their feedback on the first three chapters.

Grateful thanks to the seasoned pilots I've had the honor to fly with, whose collective wisdom and first-hand feedback have helped me refine my own aeronautical competence, awareness, and discipline: flight instructors **Charlie Hayes**, **Dave Morss**, **Jonathan Hughes**, **Jim Britton**, **Brett Hinze**, **Mark Montague**, **Robert Stone**, **Quest Richlife**, **Paul Corbett**, & **Dale Masters**, as well as informal mentors **Matt Gillis**, **Harry Fox**, **Daniel Ruegemer**, **Haven Rich**, **Kurt Thams**, & **Jeff Gooding**. Also deserving a nod are the authors of reference books I've consulted time and again: **Russell Holtz** (*Flight Training Manual for Gliders* and *Glider Pilot's Handbook of Aeronautical Knowledge*) & **Wolfgang Langewiesche** (*Stick and Rudder: An Explanation of the Art of Flying*).

Heartfelt thanks to all the passengers who have entrusted me with their life and allowed me to share with them the joy of the sky, especially my first guest **Christopher Pedregal**, and my mother **Marie Christiane Zahil-Karam** who has never wavered in her support for my flying endeavors ever since I revealed to her that I had become a pilot.

9 780997 355307